*JOSÉ ORTEGA Y GASSET*

*Modern Literature Monographs*

○○○○○○○○○○○○○○○○○○○○○○○○○○○○○○○○○○○○○○○○○○○○○

# JOSÉ ORTEGA
# Y GASSET

*Franz Niedermayer*

Translated by Peter Tirner

*Frederick Ungar Publishing Co.*
*New York*

Translated from the original German and published by arrangement with Colloquium Verlag, Berlin. New material and revisions for the American edition were prepared by the author.

*Contents*

○○○○○○○○○○○○○○○○○○○○○○○○○○○○○○○○○○○○○○○○○○○○○○○

# *Chronology*

1883: José Ortega y Gasset is born in Madrid on 9 May.

1891–96: Attends Jesuit school at Málaga.

1898: At the University of Salamanca takes first-year examination, which is conducted by Miguel de Unamuno. A friendship develops between the two men.
Spain is defeated in Spanish-American War.

1899: Ortega passes required annual examination at the Central University of Madrid.

1902: Passes final required examination with grade "excellent." Makes his first mark as a journalist with "Critique of Criticism."

1904: Is granted degree from the Central University of Madrid with his dissertation "The Terrors of the Year 1000." Becomes engaged to Rosa Spottorno-Topete. Makes his first visit to Germany.

1905–07: Makes visits to Leipzig, Berlin, and Marburg, where he studies with the neo-Kantian philosopher Hermann Cohen.

1908: Is appointed to the faculty of the Escuela Superior de Magisterio.

1909:   On 15 October strongly criticizes the Spanish government in a speech at the Ateneo in Madrid. Cabinet resigns a week later.

1910:   Makes speech in honor of the first socialist representative. On 7 April marries Rosa Spottorno-Topete.

1910–36:   Holds the position, with interruptions, of professor of metaphysics at the Central University of Madrid.

1911:   Studies with Hermann Cohen at Marburg. His first son, Miguel Germán, is born in May.

1914:   Publishes *Meditations on Quixote*. Makes speech against the government. Is elected to the Academia de Ciencias Morales y Políticas. His daughter, Soledad, is born.

1915–16:   Becomes a driving force in the new weekly *España*.

1916:   Takes trip to Buenos Aires. His second son, José, is born.

1916–35:   Publishes his one-man review, *El Espectador*.

1920:   Publishes series of articles in *El Sol*.

1922:   *Invertebrate Spain* is published. Becomes general editor of The Library of Twentieth-Century Ideas, published by Espasa-Calpe.

1923:   *The Modern Theme* is published.

1923–36:   Publishes the journal *Revista de Occidente*.

1924:   Writes essay on the occasion of the two-hundredth anniversary of Kant's birth.

1925:   *The Dehumanization of Art* and *Notes on the Novel* are published.

1928:   Goes on lecture tour to Argentina.

1929:   Holds lecture series "What Is Philosophy?" in Madrid.

1930:   *Revolt of the Masses* is published.

1931: The second Spanish republic is declared. Ortega is elected as a delegate to the legislature.

1932: Publishes *Mission of the University*.

1934: Again visits Germany.

1935: Five essays on Germany are published in Buenos Aires. Ortega receives Gold Medal of Madrid.

1936: Miguel de Unamuno dies on 31 December.

1936–39: Civil war is fought in Spain.

1936–48: Ortega spends exile in France, the Netherlands, South America, and Portugal.

1940: Is elected *in absentia* as a member of the Consejo de la Hispanidad.

1946: The first edition of Ortega's collected works is published.

1948: Returns to Spain, gives lectures at the Instituto de Humanidades.

1949: Visits the United States and Germany, where he participates in the celebrations for the two-hundredth anniversary of Goethe's birth.

1951–52: Pays frequent visits to Germany.

1955: Ortega dies in Madrid on 18 October. A special memorial service is held at the University of Madrid on 18 November.

○○○○○○○○○○○○○○○○○○○○○○○○○○○○○○○○○○○○○○○○○○○○○○

# *By Way*
# *of a Preface*

*In general*:

Any man studying *las cosas de España* must be an Hispano-
phile, just as I become an Italophile whenever I study
Italian culture.

*—Karl Vossler to Benedetto Croce, in a letter of 25 August*
*1933*

What we French consider the quest for truth, the Spanish
consider an error.

*—Blaise Pascal*

Nobody who is not himself a Spaniard can ever please
Spain's natives when writing about Spain. . . . Accordingly,
the Spaniards will hardly accept as valid what I here have to
say. But I can only set down what I saw, and what lives on
within me as the fruit of what I saw.

*—Hermann Keyserling*

*In particular*:

There could be no greater mistake than to base a biography
of Don José Ortega y Gasset strictly on the factual data of

1

his life. This writer has no history. His life is imbedded in his works, has been shaped by his thought. The history of his thought, the study of his works, require the support of no more than a minimum of vital statistics.

—CORPUS BARGA, *in 1933, on Ortega y Gasset*

You will no doubt write many books in future, even good books. But that is not the point; that is just something you can *do*. Your real task, it seems to me, would still be this: some time or other, you must present to us what a man *is*.

—*Georg Simmel to his student Hermann Keyserling (about 1906), and thus indirectly to Keyserling's friend and rival Ortega*

The first and last of these quotations are offered as the true *leitmotif* of this book.

"Spaniards make history; they do not talk about it." Or, as Father Feijóo of the eighteenth century described Spaniards: "They all took up the sword, not one took up the pen."

In fact, far fewer personal memoirs are published in Spain than in other western-European countries. In 1936, Ortega promised that he would write his autobiography; he never did. When he died, he left behind a large debit of philosophical and autobiographical works announced but never written. Most of the books he published are not real books, as he himself admitted, but were collections of journal articles, or occasional features that had appeared in Spanish and South American newspapers, put together at the suggestion of a publisher. Yet even his more general publications invariably contain traces of his personal life and references to his state of mind and way of life at the time of the writing. In addition, more so than the writings of most other thinkers, they are an expression of the times. Thus, much of Ortega's life story is available to us. His writings may be regarded both as a kind of diary and as the testimonial of an adventurous soul. "Every one of these pages summed up my whole existence at the hour when it was written; all of them put together represent the melody of my life," he wrote in the foreword to the first edition of his collected works.

Gregorio Marañón, in his funeral oration for Ortega in November 1955, was to voice the same idea.

In 1932, Ortega confessed: "Fortunately, I still find the idea of writing my memoirs peculiarly revolting . . . I look back to the past without enthusiasm. . . ." What he called "the dumb stupidity of tracks in the sand" did not interest him. His scholarly and scientific pursuits, his personal habits, his nomadic life—everything militated against his writing a self-portrait. But even if he had done so, the time would not have been ripe for publishing memoirs. Our age is not yet calm and detached enough to accept all the paradoxes and challenges that such a work would be certain to contain.

The only resource left to Ortega's biographer, then, is to laboriously put into order what data he can retrieve from Ortega's published works. "The reason biography is always like a game of chance played in the realm of intuition is that there is no sure method to unlock a stranger's inner being with a secret key," Ortega wrote in 1932. In Ortega's view, the man who evaluates oversimplifies and thereby falsifies living reality. Although we cannot completely avoid oversimplification with its inherent falsification, we do not want to go so far in this as to lose our grasp on reality. To my knowledge, no complete and up-to-date biography of Ortega has been written. In Spain, where Ortega's work is still so controversial, no one has been rash enough to attempt such a task.

I am aware that there are many who will deny a non-Spaniard the right to speak on Ortega. But I feel that I can perform a necessary service by presenting the Ortega whom the non-Spanish world has yet to discover: the Spaniard who was the representative of a troubled people and of their special character; the man rooted in Spain's turbulent history, and standing in its very vortex. The man who thus emerges is much to be preferred to the stereotypes of Ortega the itinerant preacher or Ortega the universal wiseacre. A citizen of Europe by an act of will, Spaniard by nature and by temperament, Ortega, throughout his life (with the exception perhaps of the last five years), strove with everything he did to leave his mark on his country, in intellectual as well as political matters. I shall focus especially on the unknown Ortega, the political man who has so often been misrepresented and is in need of vindication.

Once we achieve an understanding of Ortega's life, we shall understand the essence of his philosophy. In this regard, Ortega is in complete agreement with another great philosopher of the Latin world, the social critic and Germanophile Benedetto Croce, who said: "True philosophy must be lived!" He is like Socrates, Plato, Augustine, Nicholas of Cusa, and Pascal. Ortega, who was fond of using phrases minted by the Catholic Church, and who in fact endowed such phrases with fresh luster, confirmed the trinity of philosophy, life, and politics when he said: "My life spent itself by the side of Spain's road through history like burning incense."

If Ortega's work cannot be counted among the cornerstones of Western philosophy (Marías's long-promised systematic treatment is still outstanding), it remains nonetheless an important testimonial of his time, a link that joins many modern philosophical systems and provides a new and final synthesis for some of them.

Above all else, the life of Ortega y Gasset is authentically Spanish. He is part and parcel of that insoluble Spanish riddle, which, in Friedrich Nietzsche's words, is "perhaps the greatest riddle that there is in the European tradition," because "this people has made the most radical transition from wanting to be too much, to too much wanting not to be." A nation that has once been the first among nations—can it again be as it was, or must it be different? In Spain this existential problem has been hotly debated for more than a century, not only among scholars but also among poets, journalists, politicians, and indeed all educated people. It is the problem that is at the heart of the dichotomy between "two Spains" (the one political, the other philosophical), which, for the last century and a half, has caused civil war and dethronement, dynastic feud, emigration, and imprisonment.

Spain's decline as a political power beginning in the seventeenth century, the loss of her colonies in 1898, the political interventions of the French and English in the eighteenth and nineteenth centuries, and of the Germans, Italians, Russians, and Americans in the twentieth: these events constitute the embarrassing yet inescapable background against which the nation's self-examination and its persistent internal strife are carried on. They are the facts that prompted even Ortega, notwithstanding all his intelligence, worldly wisdom, and understanding of human nature, to enter "politics, which means to have a clear conception of what the state must do to shape a nation."

The conflicts, which erupted into the open around 1800, had existed, of course, for more than three centuries, though in the form of ideological clashes within Spain's ruling class. "We must make a new start!" the progressive minister of state Pedro Pablo Abarca de Bolea, Conde de Aranda, had exclaimed in the eighteenth century. His adherents are to this day known as the *progresistas*. In the cultural sphere, they were called *ilustrados* in the eighteenth and *liberales* in the nineteenth century. In the twentieth century those with similar viewpoints are known as the *modernistas*. Their opponents, the *tradicionalistas*, cry: "We must turn back!" Let us march in the footsteps of Philip II, Charles V, and El Cid.

About a hundred years ago, in reaction to the threatening idolization of throne and altar by the *tradicionalistas* with their conservative nostalgia for the

past, the *europeizantes* (those who want to open Spain
to European culture) arose. Ortega was to become
their most important representative in Spain's history.
Accordingly, we cannot count among his spiritual ancestors such conservative thinkers as the Catalan Jaime
Luciano Balmes, nor the brilliant theologian and historian Donoso Cortés, and least of all the polymath
and strictly orthodox thinker Menéndez y Pelayo. In
fact, though he preceded him in time, Menéndez y Pelayo (1856–1912) must be regarded as Ortega's true
antagonist.

Ortega's spiritual ancestors are the reformers.
They were the men who had turned their eyes toward
central Europe, and had raised new and strange gods
upon their altars: not Kant, Fichte, and Schelling, but
the obscure founder of panentheism (the doctrine that
God includes the world as a part though not the whole
of his being) named Karl Christian Friedrich Krause
(1781–1832), who borrowed something from each of
these three great thinkers, and mixed the pilferings together in a concoction of his own. Brought back from
central Europe by some imprudent pilgrims, this im-
portation began to ferment and produced the brew of
Spanish *krausismo*—a new sort of romantic-humanistic-
areligious mysticism for the layman. "An exceedingly
droll spectacle" was Ortega's comment on it. "Excellent people and very poor performers" he called these
bizarre *krausistas,* who initiated and embraced a movement surely without precedent and without serious
consequences, but not without side effects. Despite the
opposition of the government and of the clergy, the
*krausistas* established excellent private schools, they
gained control of the universities, and controlled the
award of grants for study abroad. Ortega himself, in
his youth, became one of their beneficiaries. He re-

vered their leader, Francisco Giner de los Ríos, as if he were a new saint; he equally revered the socialist idealist Pablo Iglesias. Their leading metaphysician, Nicolas Salmerón (1838-1908), was for a brief time (1873) President of the first Spanish republic, and Ortega's predecessor at the Central University of Madrid.

The goal of these well-intentioned but erratic social reformers was to raise Spain "to the level of the times." Ortega agreed with this goal, but found that he had more to learn from the Generation of '98 than from the *krausistas*. The '98ers, a group of young men of great literary talent, among whom were Azorín, Pío Baroja y Nessi, and Miguel de Unamuno, were deeply shaken by Spain's defeat in the Spanish-American War and the internal weakness and aimlessness within Spain. By means of thinking and writing, they hoped to discover a cure for Spain's malaise, to find their bearings, and to reassess Spain's situation. What they accomplished was "a lot of literature, a little philosophy, some theology, scant science." Ortega himself is frequently considered among the group, though he should not be. Not only was he younger than they were, but he was unlike the '98ers in many ways. Undoubtedly the greatest of the so-called Sons of the '98ers, he was more modern, more industrious, more comprehensive in learning, more scientific, more experienced in worldly affairs, and more influential than the '98ers. The '98ers were at heart provincial enthusiasts, passivists, high-minded poets and dreamers. Ortega was to become the teacher and leader of the so-called Grandsons of the '98ers, those men now in their sixties who have achieved positions that enable them to exert influence in present-day Spain or are trying to get such positions. Becoming Spain's leading expert on Europe, his influence in that role was unequalled be-

dowment, temperament. They held in common an admiration for France and England and, later and less
unanimously, for Germany as well, the countries in
which they had spent their apprentice years together.
But in the end, the lessons they would draw from
those years were to differ widely.

Ortega's own remark, "I was born on a rotary press," has been widely quoted. For generations the Ortega family had been connected with the printed word; he was expected to follow in this path. His friends urged the gifted youth to go out into the world and face the greater challenges of philosophy. But in his heart of hearts he knew that he would never belong to philosophy alone. His paternal grandfather had been the founder of *Imparcial,* the leading Madrid newspaper. His father was one of the paper's contributors as well as editor-in-chief of its important Monday edition. His mother's family, the Gassets, were also publishers. One member of the family was the king's minister of state. Ortega himself shared his father's liking for the newspaper world and his interest in politics. He inherited the family's liberal tradition, their talent for languages, and their love of travel.

José Ortega y Gasset was born in Madrid on 9 May 1883, the second son among four children. The family lived on Alfonso XII, the quiet and elegant street that borders Retiro Park. All through the year, young José could enjoy the freedom and variety of city life, or roam the park's winding paths under tall trees and walk in the fragrant splendor of the celebrated rose gardens.

But the most dearly treasured memories of his childhood, those that he would speak of in later years with true enthusiasm, were those of attending school (1891 to 1896) at Málaga. All three of the Ortega brothers were educated at Miraflores del Palo, a new and well-run Jesuit school. José formed many lasting friendships with his Jesuit teachers, who recognized and encouraged his exceptional gifts. Years later, thinking back to those days, he would still see himself as the "emperor of the radiant realm of the eastern

14

shore"; a deep passion for light and sunshine, for clarity and beauty in life, remained with him through all
his years and became the guiding principle of his
thinking as well. He excelled in his studies, was
awarded high marks even for behavior, was never ill.
Like his father, Ortega was trained by priests—and
like his father, he outgrew them at an early age. As
Ignazio Silone said once, "The liveliest freethinkers
have always come from Jesuit colleges." Among Ortega's contemporaries, the remark would apply to the
great novelist from the north Ramón Pérez de Ayala,
and to Nobel Prize poet Juan Ramón Jiménez from
the south of Spain.

Graciela Palau de Nemes's biography of Jiménez
(*Life and Works of Juan Ramón Jiménez,* 1957) provides us with certain further details about those school
years that Ortega never commented upon: the educational mistakes typical of the times and the ideological
gaps that prompted all three—Pérez de Ayala, Jiménez,
Ortega—to turn their backs on Roman Catholicism.
The method of teaching philosophy prevalent in those
days—teaching that was mechanical and formalistic, a
rote drill in scholasticism—is not likely to have encouraged lasting religious faith. A parallel situation in Ireland prompted James Joyce, also a pupil of the Jesuits,
to free himself from the religion of his youth and to
become a eulogist of life.

Things must be different in Spain today, if we
may judge by the otherwise depressing autobiography
of the young Spanish emigrant Michel de Castillo, entitled *Tanguy,* which pays such radiant tribute to his
Jesuit headmaster Father Pardo of Úbeda. Today,
even the work of the somewhat heretical Unamuno is
being read and discussed in class, as is the work of
other nonconformists such as Azorín and Baroja y

Nessi. In Ortega's days, the works of the lively French writer Ernest Renan may have served the same purpose—to stimulate independent thinking in the students—for Ortega said of them that they had "accompanied me from my childhood on," as a "refreshment of the spirit." Soon Ortega would add the works of the rebellious Friedrich Nietzsche from whom he got his first taste of German philosophy. The objections of the once influential Menéndez y Pelayo to the "Germanic mists" did not stand up to Ortega's close scrutiny.

José Ortega graduated young, returning to live in his beloved native city of Madrid, to which he was devoted. The ambience of the fast-moving and resplendent city was the very stuff of life to him; away from it he was never fully himself. In fact, the difference between the two greatest Spanish thinkers of this century, Ortega and Unamuno, can best be understood through their contrasting attitudes toward Madrid. Unamuno, the brooding, eccentric Basque, thought Madrid "terrible—it offers neither company nor nature; you can have neither privacy nor any true communication." Useful acquaintances could be made quickly there, he admitted, but only rarely did a Madrid man open his heart to any of his fellow human beings.

It seems significant that the first encounter between these two men, the Spanish intellectual giants of their day, should take place at the University of Salamanca, seat of Spain's classical tradition. It was in Salamanca that Unamuno had chosen to make his home. While studying at the Jesuit College of Deusto near Bilbao, Ortega in 1898 had to report to Salamanca for his examination. He acquitted himself well in the examination, conducted by Miguel de Unamuno, professor of Greek, a man of broad interests.

Indeed, Ortega seems to have left a lasting impression on him. It was not long before they were exchanging letters and planning joint projects. Thus began the slowly maturing, lifelong friendship between two great minds, punctuated by high-minded competition and sharp clashes. The year 1898 was the year of Spain's military defeat. It was also the year that witnessed the emergence of a group of young militant intellectuals, who became known as the Generation of '98. Within the group (whose very existence as an intellectual community has often been contested) Ortega found his political mentor in Joaquín Costa, Spain's gadfly, who in one of his writings called for "Spain's restoration and Europeanization" by way of "schools and larders" (*escuelas y despensas*). Costa demanded that the tomb of El Cid, and with it all of Spain's romantic tradition, be put out of sight for good. After Costa's death, Ortega was to continue this "patriotic housecleaning."

What was the impression Ortega left on his fellow students at school? We have the report of Vicente Pereda, son of José Maria de Pereda (the author of the novel *Up into the Mountains*), as it is quoted by González Caminero in his essay "Ortega Posthumously":

Ortega was at that time a young man of average height, with penetrating eyes, extraordinary intelligence, and superior demeanor. We met regularly in the cell of Father Gonzalo Coloma. Here Ortega developed, among other things, his enthusiasm for G. A. Bécquer (Spain's greatest late Romantic) and Bécquer's swallows. Even then he showed great gifts for astute criticism, as well as a literary bent, both of which were to stay with him for a long time, perhaps all his life. . . . As a student he showed great facility, and distinguished himself without effort. But he was always generous toward his fellow students, indeed wholly without competitive envy or arrogance. The fact was that

he was extremely talented; his excellent memory stood him
in good stead; he handled every assignment with enviable
self-confidence and assurance. His spirit overflowed with
youthful romanticism, superbly complemented by his great
intellectual discipline and good planning. His budding
curiosity drew him in all directions, his character was that
of a cheerful youngster. He never took part in sports, or in
noisy empty chatter, and this drew us together. Famous
names of ancient nobility did not impress him, nor did
religious ceremonial. At his core even then was his critical
disposition, though concealed under the outward practices
that controlled him.

In 1899, Ortega passed the required annual examination in Madrid, at the country's leading university.
But the Central University of Madrid could not cap-
ture the talented young man's imagination. "A dirty
building without personality," he called it, situated
on the narrow and twisting Calle de San Bernardo.
Teachers and students without individuality or stature, all faceless shadows in the eyes of this young man
of great promise. At the moment he was pursuing
studies in jurisprudence and the humanities; no special interest had yet made itself felt. He gathered
around him a circle of high-minded friends, all good
patriots, many of them considerably more conservative
and traditionalist than he, who was an admirer of
French positivism.

Later, Ortega was to speak of these years as his
"sentimental years," because it was then that he
courted his future wife. When the hot summer came
to the city, he fled to the cool slopes of the Guadar-
rama mountains. It was there that he first read and
struggled with the works of Immanuel Kant.

His examination in 1902, passed with the grade
"excellent," opened the way for his dissertation, com-

pleted in 1904, on a humanistic-historical theme, "The Terrors of the Year 1000." In it he examined the manifestations in France of that universal doomsday mood called chiliasm. Later, Ortega would not allow this dissertation to be included in his collected works. The "son of the rotary press" also made his first mark as a journalist with a literary "Critique of Criticism" (1902), an analysis of his literary exemplars, the French. Before becoming involved in political issues, a concern that would stay with him all his life, diverting him from the straight and narrow path of professional specialization, he was seized by an aesthetic tension, fascinated by questions of taste and style, and all the problems arising from Spain's shift toward the artistic movement of "modernism." Ortega was as much an artist as a political man, an aesthetician even more than an existentialist. The short essays he wrote during his vacations in northern and western Spain, or his sketches of important visitors to Madrid (Maurice Maeterlinck, for example, or the Cartusian monks that came from Cordoba, or Spanish poets) captured the scenes with great skill. From the very start Ortega stood forth as a master of literary style and as a great journalist. With his friend and political rival Maeztu, Ortega would set a new standard for journalism throughout Spain.

Ortega and Maeztu, enthusiastic Nietzscheans at the time, launched many a caper by arrogating to themselves the privileges of the "superman." The visiting Maeterlinck, for example, felt strongly attracted by the great Spanish mystics; the Nietzschean Ortega, at that time an admirer also of Thomas Carlyle, promptly rejected their writings as "hallucinations from the beyond." Juan Marichal has given us a good portrait of the young Ortega, whom he described as

"the scion of a distinguished family, constantly in revolt, and ceaselessly enthusiastic," a young man brim-
ming with revolt against the *fin de siècle,* enthusiasm
for a new beginning for Spain and for the world. But
Ortega was in danger of getting stuck in a journalistic
rut, as Maeztu did, and of frittering his great gifts
away. He was never to escape entirely from this pitfall,
despite the later academic appointments.

Ortega was moulded as a writer by the French
masters. He believed that the road to a country's preeminence was based on economic and intellectual pro-
ductivity and power. Thus he went to study in Germany when Wilhelm II was emperor. Looking back to
that period later, in 1934, he compared himself to a
young hawk, "ravenous, proud, and warlike," who
flies forth hunting for "living flesh" to bring back to
his ruined Spanish castle. "I studied deeply, furiously,
without reserve, without bounds. For three years, I
was a pure Celto-Iberian flame blazing with enthusiasm in the German universities." Among the outstanding young men of Ortega's generation whom the
state-supported Junta for Extended Study sent abroad
were such men as Eugenio D'Ors and Pérez de Ayala,
who went to Munich, and Marañón, who went to
Frankfurt. Not one *grande tour,* however, was more
fruitful for Spain and for Germany than was that of
Ortega. His first trip, in 1904, was followed in 1905
by his first visit to Germany's seats of learning. In
Leipzig he began to study German and to work on
Kant. These studies were carried on during long walks
in the Zoological Garden or on the snowy paths of the
surrounding Rosenthal as well as at other times. Max
Funke, an ambitious young scientist, became his con-
stant companion.

An excursion took Ortega to Nuremburg, an industrial town steeped in tradition, and prompted him to raise the question: Would it ever be possible in far-away Spain, in Toledo or Cordoba, to integrate history and art and modern industry in this fashion?

In 1906 and 1907 Ortega, by grace of the Junta for Extended Study, continued his studies in Berlin. But no truly great minds awaited him there. Wilhelm Dilthey, who would have been a kindred spirit, was by then *emeritus;* Berlin's libraries had more to offer him than Berlin's lecture halls. Ortega was later to lament that his failure to meet Dilthey had cost him ten years of philosophical struggle. There was only Georg Simmel, a man of wide-ranging interests, who introduced him to the vastness and vitality of philosophical thought.

The exchange rate of the Spanish peseta was then so low that Ortega could only rarely afford to eat in restaurants, even if only to treat himself to beer and knockwurst at the popular students' haunt, Aschinger's Brewery.

Ortega felt strongly attracted to what was then the European philosopher's Mecca, the little town of Marburg, center of the neo-Kantian Hermann Cohen, Paul Natorp, and Rudolf Stammler. Years later, the woods around the Escorial would recall those days in Marburg to Ortega's mind: "a small gothic town by a quiet dark river among the gently rolling hills covered with dense fir and beech forests. It is the town where I spent the equinox of my youth; the town to which I owe half of my hopes and nearly all of my intellectual discipline. The town is Marburg on the Lahn River."

Hermann Cohen, aged but still imposing, became Ortega's mentor and friend, while Natorp's reading of Plato impressed Ortega less. Among his age group his two special friends were Nicolai Hartmann and Heinz Heimsoeth.

Ortega's early years in Germany, the first two of many, were followed by outstanding work when he returned to Spain. His written and oral work earned him a faculty appointment at the Escuela Superior de Magisterio, established in 1908. He taught psychology, ethics, and logic. This first professional assignment eminently suited the young Ortega, because he was convinced that the solution of the "Spanish problem," the problem of an "intellectually dead race," had to be worked out in the area of education. Every Spaniard, Ortega insisted, should study the sciences. Nor did Ortega shy away from open polemics. He attacked not only Menéndez y Pelayo, the elder statesman of the Catholic-oriented cultural movement, but his own friend Maeztu, then press correspondent in London, and even Prime Minister Antonio Maura: "My liberalism prompts me to consider Europe more important than Spain, which, after all, is only one part of Europe."

Among Spain's artists, Ortega preferred the tough and realistic painter Ignacio Zuloaga to the lighter and more optimistic Joaquín Sorolla. That same attitude drew Ortega even then toward the world of politics. The guiding motto of his life was to be a line from Seneca, the first philosopher of stature of the Iberian peninsula: *vivere militare est!* (to live is to fight!). He rejected Nietzsche's "live dangerously!" in favor of Ariosto's more sober *vivere risolutamente!* (live resolutely).

For a period of about six months the Madrid weekly *Faro* became the mouthpiece of the activist Ortega. On 15 October 1909, in Madrid's intellectual center, the Ateneo, Ortega made a public speech sharply attacking the Spanish government: within the week, the cabinet resigned. To Ortega, none of the old parties seemed satisfactory, and even the liberals, he felt, would have to reform.

In 1908 the German art historian Julius Meier-Graefe came to Spain to trace the sources of impressionism—and to discover El Greco for the European art world. Meier-Graefe was annoyed with this young Spaniard who spoke German fluently and knew Germany so well, who had such high regard for German laboratories and German military display, German organization and German institutions, but who considered Imperial Germany, in Meier-Graefe's words, "a comfort station of a higher order." Ortega declined to voice an opinion about German scholarship, or spoke evasively, but was sufficiently voluble in his admiration for Goethe (whose influence was to become one of the strongest streams in Ortega's world view). When Meier-Graefe questioned him about "popish rule" and "intolerance" in Spain, Ortega was able to reassure him by announcing that he himself, known to the authorities as a "socialist," would shortly obtain a faculty appointment, as indeed he did, at the teacher's college.

In 1909, Ortega lectured in the socialist Casa del Pueblo on the subject "Science and Religion as Political Problems." In 1910 he celebrated Spain's first socialist deputy as a "new saint." But this occasional partisanship did not imply that the politically idealistic Ortega had made a binding decision; it merely meant that he was opposed to the ruling clique.

Meier-Graefe's visit gave Ortega the opening to express his views of Germany in the Madrid newspapers. He distinguished "two Germanies": one, the country of intellectual labors, as exemplified by the philosophers Leibniz and Kant, and the pathologist

Rudolf Virchow; the other, the materialist and imperialist land of Wilhelm II, in which (according to Ortega) science and scholarship subserved political power, music was nationalist, literature hypocritical, and even painting unrealistic, cloying, and debilitating. In 1910, Ortega's review of Meier-Graefe's book about his Spanish visit appeared under the title "Arrogance as a Literary Genre." I will only point out that Meier-Graefe, unable to speak Spanish, did not come to understand the true Spain, his admiration for El Greco notwithstanding.

The year 1910 marked a high point in Ortega's life: on 7 April after six years of courtship, he married Rosa Spottorno-Topete. The marriage, which would be blessed with three children, may truly be called a happy one, a source of comfort for this man so sorely tried by fate.

In November of 1910 Ortega was appointed professor of metaphysics at the Central University of Madrid. His victory over four other aspirants owed something to the presence of kindred spirits among the scholars in charge of the appointment but was principally due to his own incontestable merit. Because of his concern about education, he continued for a considerable length of time to hold his professorship at the teachers' college, without a salary.

The appointment of the twenty-seven-year-old Ortega, bursting with energy, to one of Spain's most important professorships (it would soon be *the* decisive faculty position) was a portentous departure for a nation that British Prime Minister Lord Salisbury had called "mortally ill." It seems appropriate to recall here that in 1910 Ortega remarked: "For a man born anywhere between the Bidasoa and Gibraltar, Spain is the first, the whole, the perduring problem."

Under many pseudonyms and using a variety of literary forms, Ortega wrote a number of reports on Spain's political and intellectual situation. The series was called *Salvaciones,* because these were to be, Ortega hoped, signposts along Spain's road to salvation. As early as 1910 Ortega, as a true disciple of Natorp, raised his voice on matters of practice, method, policy, and on social education as a political problem. He advocated a social ethic in the form of an intellectualized socialism, and the gradual elimination of religious teaching, leading to a "free" morality in a secular school system. Spain, the problem; Europe, the solution! He was merciless in his criticism of the feeble and aimless state of the nation. The activist Ortega became a politicized educator, a totally political man.

His appointment to a key academic position brought a tremendous response from the nation's young intelligentsia; after all, he was one of their most promising members! His "elder brother in spirit" (older by eight years) Maeztu, now back from England, rejoiced that from now on no one in Spain would be able to earn a higher academic degree without knowing Kant, and called for "five hundred more Ortegas!" In December of 1910, one hundred and fifty friends and admirers gathered at a banquet in Madrid to honor Ortega. They celebrated his scholarly preeminence without envy. Ortega's appointment was indeed an event of national importance, one whose significance for the development of an intellectual elite in Spain would grow from year to year, at least until 1936.

Thus began a quarter century of teaching and intellectual leadership, the most productive period in Ortega's life. It had been preceded by another stay in Germany, his third. His last term of study abroad was financed by a government grant. Accompanied by his young wife, Ortega spent a year, from January to December of 1911, with

the great Hermann Cohen. I shall never forget those summer evenings, their dark skies full of flickering stars, when I walked to the master's house and found him bending over our book (*Don Quixote*), which he read in Tieck's translation. He would raise his aged and noble head and greet me with the words: "Just look, your Sancho constantly has on his lips the very word that is the cornerstone of Fichte's philosophy."

Ortega helped Cohen to work out his aesthetics.

When his first son was born, in May, Ortega named him Miguel in honor of Miguel de Cervantes, Spain's greatest writer, "a lowly and poor Spaniard who wandered the roads of the world and under his most courteous smile concealed a heart burdened with deep sorrow." Miguel

was born in the flowering month of May, on the feastday of the holy Germanus. And so I called him Miguel Germán. Michel is the name that typefies the German rooted in his native soil, who still lives on that soil, lives on and by its fruits, the breed of rustic man that is the rich soil by which the whole nation is sustained.

Even in his most personal concerns, indeed, especially in these, Ortega remained the loyal son of his own, beloved people. But this selection of name is also evidence of his frequently shown "honest, deep, passionate enthusiasm for Germany's destiny, concern for her fears."

In Germany, Ortega discussed Kant and Parmenides with Hartmann, Heimsoeth, and Scheffer. He also listened on occasion to the melancholy cello music of Hartmann, that great son of the Baltic region who would soon smash the ring of neo-Kantian scholasticism, escape the narrow, rigid group of thinkers. Ortega would in time follow in Hartmann's footsteps, but in his own Spanish fashion.

One of his rare visits to Italy brought Ortega to Florence. The impressions gathered on that journey may be what prompted him to write a lengthy essay on a theme remote from his main interests, Leonardo da Vinci's *Mona Lisa:* an essay written in Marburg, Germany, about an Italian painting recently come from Paris, for publication in a Spanish journal! Surely the event augured well for the future citizen of Europe. A print of the *Mona Lisa* later graced the wall of Ortega's study, together with an El Greco.

Ortega's journalistic leanings caused him to contribute also to the Madrid newspaper *Imparcial* and to two other publications. In the pages of these periodicals he expressed his preference for the French *écrivain* (a type closely akin to him) over the typical and much admired German scholar, and gave vent to his "spontaneous dislike for Germanic culture" because of its "Protestant pathos, pedantry, poverty of intuition, artistic and literary insensitivity, qualities that the average German displays equally prominently in politics" (September 1911). And yet, he wrote, Spain can make progress only by means of German scholarship and science. It cannot reach the *vida esencial* in any other way. He had brought from Germany, he wrote, "a new and superb nourishment" to his starved Spanish country. He had studied German methods and institutions in behalf of his fellow Spaniards. This deep respect for matters German also enabled him to warn his fellow Spaniards against the traditional weaknesses of the German nation and, among other things, against the first signs of rising antisemitism. Ortega's

keen mind discerned even then, in Wilhelm II's empire, what the total disjunction between spirit and
power portended.

When Ortega returned to Spain with wife and
child, his Spanish friends and fellow students did not
know what to admire him most for—as "a tremendous
mind, a savant" (thus Maeztu), as "an artist through
and through" (thus Araquistain), as "a perfect saint."
Still other observers noted Ortega's extraordinary sen-
sitivity, and an extraordinary will to dominate. Indeed, his personal ambition may have been as great as
his exceptional gifts.

An estrangement between him and the revered
Dean of Salamanca, Miguel de Unamuno, nearly
twenty years his senior, was thus inevitable. In one of
the many letters that Ortega wrote, while studying in
Germany in 1907, to the most distinguished and most
self-willed member of the Generation of '98, were the
words: "I am very lonesome, and need the Ariadne-
thread of your friendship to find my way out of this
labyrinth of labors, cares, and studies." But the friendship had begun to weaken. Unamuno refused to move
to Madrid, although Ortega, now very influential,
thought he could succeed in having him offered a
chair in the philosophy of religion at the Central University (a post to be newly established) "at a top salary." Nor would Unamuno accept the warnings
against Nietzsche and other "modern mystics" that Ortega, whose philosophical education was superior to
that of Unamuno, urged upon him.

In vain Ortega traveled to Salamanca to enlist
Unamuno's support for a political movement of Spanish renewal and reform. Unamuno declined to become
"the father of a movement whose holy spirit emanates
from Ortega." Despite their common patriotism, de-

spite the journalistic collaboration that arose from it, a breach between the two men became inevitable because of their fundamental disagreement on basic issues. It occurred when Unamuno, in an open letter to Azorín, once again exalted mysticism above scientific knowledge, which amounted to an attack by the country's most respected thinker on Ortega's own efforts in the service of scientific research, and on his plans for founding a Spain in which self-disciplined intelligence prevailed.

In this clash is to be seen the collision of two generations, two different levels of intellectual formation, two styles of thinking, two different ideals of national reform. The older man, *actor* and *sentidor,* doer and man of intuition, was very different from the younger *cientifico* and *espectador,* man of science and observer. It was not until decades later, decades spent both in mutual understanding and in mutual opposition, like Voltaire and Rousseau, that the two men met again, on the eve of the Spanish civil war, which they, knowingly or unknowingly, had helped to bring about. But the writings of the two, who vied with each other for the nation's attention, are to this day the favorite reading of Spain's student generation. Unamuno's appeal lay in his depth, his religious fervor, his passion, and in his Spanish-ness. Ortega drew readers to him on the basis of his lucid and balanced style, his philosophical and scientific thought.

In his famous novel *Troteras y danzaderas* (1912), Ramón Pérez de Ayala has left us a sensitive portrait of Ortega in the description of Tejero:

a young professor of philosophy, with a certain aura of the politician. His personality and his still immature ideas had earned him the devotion of a tribe of hotheaded followers. Though all his philosophical writings put together still came to no more than a small sheaf of budding ideas, this slim bundle had secured for him the admiration of many, the envy of not a few, and the respect of all. Respect denotes a sentiment that must be valued very highly, one that is harder to inspire in people than admiration. The young philosopher on occasion betrayed a tendency to make very broad and delightfully vacuous statements. He was, besides, much given to enthusiasm and, like all enthusiasts, incapable of deep emotion. Because he had a truly extraordinary literary talent, he was inclined to clothe his thoughts in witty and paradoxical aphorisms. In consequence he was at times accused of expressing himself obscurely. For example, he had described the remedy that would cure Spain's sickness in these words: "Spain will be saved on the day on which it rises to the level of a civilized nation, and that will happen when there are nine Spaniards capable of reading Plato's *Symposium* in the original language!" An admirable intellectual candor shone in his eyes, the eyes of a pure youth who could look on the spectacle of reality without suffering harm. His hairless pate, which had become bald early, was out of harmony with the youthful freshness of his eyes. The dome of his head, by its size and appearance, reminded one of Socrates, or a German. His build was unremarkable, though he was broad; his feet did not seem large but padded along as if moved by a mechanical device so that his entire body seemed to be resting on a rigid framework. He met all men with a ready friendliness, and the laughter with which he often punctuated his remarks was cordial and spirited.

Tejero-Ortega urges his friends to arrange a stirring political meeting from which he has promised himself these results: "Many, many things, tremendous things! To shake awake the conscience of the nation, to inculcate a feeling of political responsibility, to cleanse political morality. . . ." It is quite true that Ortega earnestly held these ideals, and that for decades he tried to inspire Spaniards to do likewise. But in Pérez de Ayala's novel of 1912 an opponent appears, a character of Unamuno's type who cries out to the world: "Every Spaniard is a mystic!" Men of that type have no use for German philosophy and do not take kindly to such exhortations as "Pull yourself together!"

Ortega nonetheless became the terror of the conservatives, the nemesis of superannuated politicians, and the focus of student unrest. But strange and ridiculous figures appear in his train—mindless parrots and fellow travelers, wiseacres filled with a wisdom imported from abroad. What nation has been more merciless in its self-criticism? The Russians, perhaps. Hölderlin's *Hyperion* is an example of this kind of writing in Germany. Pérez de Ayala's biting criticism of Spain at the turn of the century closes with these words: "Tejero has made fools of us!" Corruption and weakness remain in control. It may be that Pérez de Ayala did not intend so much to prophesy as to incite resistance, as Unamuno was doing, whom the German critic E. R. Curtius has celebrated as *excitator Hispaniae,* the man who aroused Spain.

Ortega threw himself into his academic tasks with all his usual verve, only to be forced quickly to realize that his students lacked the foundations that alone would allow them to climb up to the lofty heights of modern German philosophy. He, the supreme master of the Socratic method, often found himself giving lectures instead of being a participant in the Socratic dialogue for which he was aiming. His lecture in Madrid in June of 1913, at the nineteenth congress of the Asociación Española para el Progreso de las Ciencias, which he was secretary of, was addressed to an audience beyond the academic world. He talked about Hermann Cohen and Natorp, whose influence he was slow to outgrow, but he also discussed, even then, the new rising star of phenomenology, Edmund Husserl. (This address was not published until 1956.)

But his new responsibilities did not dilute the political events of the day. He took his stand against the English in the Tripoli conflict, and found himself once more at odds with his friend Maeztu.

Spain stood at the threshold of a great intellectual rejuvenation. Men of intellectual stature were making their appearance around the two friends. Among his contemporaries Ortega, a Germanophile with a European, antitraditionalist faith in science, found an ally in Eugenio D'Ors, the Catalan from the Mediterranean coast who had turned to Greek and Roman antiquity in his search for understanding. He found another in Angel Herrera, steeped in western-European Catholicism, who was to become the leader of religious modernism in Spain and the founder of the journal *El Debate*.

Great writers of the Generation of '98 continued to be heard: Azorín, Pío Baroja y Nessi, Ramón María del Valle-Inclán among them. Miguel de Unamuno preached his lay gospel throughout the land, enthusiastically proclaiming "reform, revolution, and romanticism." Unamuno's use of Germanesque alliteration was symptomatic: a love of all things German was in the air. German restaurants and bars were springing up in Madrid—the Oro del Rhin, the Heidelberg, and finally the Edelweiss, which even today is among Madrid's outstanding gourmet restaurants. Richard Wagner was celebrated, and he still is the favorite of music lovers in Barcelona, which is second only to Bayreuth in its devotion to Wagner.

But those were only the superficial side effects of Ortega's endeavors to "enrich the Spanish spirit with the torrents of the Germanic spirit." The deeper, intellectual confrontation with the issues, and the necessary separation from the neo-Kantians, occurred in his philosophical work *Meditations on Don Quixote* (*Meditaciónes del Quijote*), written in 1913 and published the next year. While bedridden at the age of seven, Ortega had within a few hours committed the first chapter of Spain's great novel to memory. Both Miguel de Cervantes and Don Quixote, the melancholy idealist familiar to every Spaniard, now served Ortega as a means of sending his own philosophy out into the world. In terms of philological scholarship, Ortega's *Meditations* offers nothing new. But it is important because it contains in a nutshell the basic elements of his philosophy. Here Ortega openly parted company with the German formalism of that time and turned to the realism of his Iberian heritage. In reacting against the idolization of culture among educated Germans, against the flight from reality among philosophers, Ortega found himself driven to a rejection, though not absolute, of both extremes, idealism and positivism. Consequently he adopted that position with which he is identified today.

Beginning with the *Meditations*, Ortega said, "all the rest of (his) labors was devoted . . . to a ceaseless struggle against utopianism," and to the advocacy of the particular value of the individual and of life, of the world of man and man's environment. Henceforth he would enter the arena as the challenger of German idealism and materialism. "Being in touch" and "love" (*conexión, amor*) were the most striking key words in the book, on which his disciple Marías wrote a detailed commentary, although it does not include any negative criticism. Life lived *sub specie temporis* rather than *sub specie aeternitatis* now became the theme of his philosophy, Ortega's "universal science of love." A number of critics, among whom is the economist Alfred Müller-Armack, have accused Ortega of idolizing life. Marías has promised to refute these criticisms by publishing a revolutionary study of Ortega, after three years of intensive research in the United States. The same work, he asserts, will also present evidence that Ortega was in fact the precursor of Martin Heidegger, a role that Ortega himself had claimed on the strength of his *Meditations.*

Ortega's fame was growing steadily. In December of 1914, the Academia de Ciencias Morales y Políticas elected him to be its twentieth member. Ortega, however, failed to respond to two invitations to deliver his inaugural address. He obviously thought it more important to address the people and to achieve recognition in the political arena, which is Spain's graduate school. In short, he gave his labors as educator of the nation precedence over his work in the universities and institutions of higher learning. No small part of those labors consisted in his frequent contributions to the cultural activities of the Residencia de Estudiantes—the famous students' house on the hill at the edge of town surrounded by a pine grove—which was the core of a movement to reform university education. His work with the students' house (where he delivered an annual lecture) caused Ortega to be branded an "enemy of the university." But such invective meant little to the proud, independent Ortega.

In the spring of 1914, Ortega delivered a telling blow against the government, and especially against the leader of the conservative faction, Antonio Maura, a blow such as Pérez de Ayala had long foreseen. In his book *Spain: A Modern History,* Salvador de Madariaga, Ortega's brother in spirit, described this proud day:

One afternoon in the month of March 1914 a youthful man with a heavy forehead, expressive eyes, and an attractive, if self-conscious, smile, came forward on the stage of the theater of La Comedia in Madrid and began to speak with quiet assurance, elegant gesture, and a finely modulated voice to a crowded house which listened eagerly, and now and then interrupted with vigorous ovations. He was the already famous professor of metaphysics of the University of Madrid, José Ortega y Gasset. But what he was explaining to this packed theater was no metaphysical question; it was the grief of his generation at the sight of what their elders had done with Spain. "Our generation," he said, "has never negotiated with the topics of patriotism, and when it hears the word Spain it does not think of Calderón and Lepanto, it does not remember the victories of The Cross, it does not call forth the vision of a blue sky, and under it a splendor—it merely feels, and that which it feels is grief." He poured scorn on what he called Official Spain. "Official Spain consists, as it were, in ghostly parties upholding ghosts of ideas which, backed by the shadows of newspapers, keep going Cabinets of hallucination. . . . The old Spain—with its governing and its governed classes, with its abuses and its usages—is now dying." The Restoration, he held, was the period when all Spain was subordinated to peace, and peace to the monarchy. The Republicans were no better, for, in their turn, by putting the Republican

ideal above peace they also forgot Spain. For him it was
necessary to kill the Restoration, since, he added, "the dead
must be thoroughly killed." And he concluded that it was
high time that everything in Spain was nationalized and
liberalized: the army, the Crown, the clergy, the workers. . . . Great hopes were raised when this body of new
men, uncontaminated by the responsibilities of the past and
the intrigues of the present, declared their intention to take
part in public life and to raise the tone and the substance
of Spanish politics.

But how to realize this high ideal of national renewal in a state under party rule, amid the power
struggles of the parliamentarians? What could a high-
minded intellectual do beyond founding another journal? Beginning in January 1915, there appeared the
weekly *España,* even more political in its orientation
than its predecessor *Faro.* For the *España,* Ortega, its
driving force, secured the collaboration of the liberal
intelligentsia of Spain, even that of his old rival Unamuno. The feuds of the past were forgotten. Unamuno
obligingly wrote on "the national will . . . with sorrow and with candor."

Before long, however, Ortega was complaining to
Unamuno about the total lack of response, and of the
insensitivity and listlessness surrounding him, while
he as the responsible editor was driving himself to the
breaking point. Still, the enterprise survived for a
year and a half. Then Ortega accepted an invitation
to Argentina, and for nine months took refuge in pure
philosophy—with Kant. The "journey to America"
proved to be a "most profound experience for a young
Spaniard."

Ortega's only daughter, Soledad, was born in
1914, his second son, José, in 1916. The low salaries
paid by Spanish institutions of higher learning com-

pelled many professors to seek some outside income. Ortega, too, had to supplement his salary by his pen; in time he became one of the very few writers in Spain who could support himself and his family by his writings.

In May of 1916, before his jaunt across the ocean, Ortega had begun to publish his famous one-man journal, *El Espectador*. In all, eight issues, of two hundred pages each, appeared at irregular intervals. The journal announced that "life in Spain compels us, whether we will or not, to political action." Yet the journal called itself the Spanish word that means spectator! The impulsiveness and lust for action of his youth are spent, gone up in smoke. In Ortega's eyes he was now a man matured by disappointment. While *El Espectador* cannot be regarded as a flight from politics, it yet marked Ortega's first step in taking a certain distance from politics. The travel writings in *El Espectador* were more than merely picturesque essays. Even Ortega's yearly summer vacations, taken with an almost ritualistic regularity, stimulated him to speculations on the state of the nation. From 1917 on, he spent his vacations almost without exception on the Basque coast in the north, in Zumaya (near San Sebastián), which became his second home. The "golden age" of Ortega the man of letters was dawning and found its expression in the short feuilletons, critiques, and essays in *El Espectador*.

Among the items Ortega published were the measured critical essays on Max Scheler's book *The Spirit of War and the German War*. These essays are among the early efforts of those who wanted to see the construction of a unified European culture. Ortega had to reprove his "great friend" Scheler for deserting Kant's *On Eternal Peace,* the same aberration he ac-

cused Henri Bergson of. Scheler was guilty of mis-
using, Ortega charged, scholarship for political ends.
In another essay he censured H. G. Wells for wholly
neglecting the socialist Ferdinand Lasalle in favor of
Karl Marx. Ortega, himself never a Marxist but a
Spanish patriot with a social conscience, held Lasalle
in high esteem. In other essays he blamed Germany
not so much for carrying World War I into neutral
Belgium as for its failure to create a new law of nations, a task for which the Germans would have been
especially well qualified in virtue of their "high cultural tradition."

In these years approving voices were now occasionally making themselves heard even among Spain's
priesthood, which was, in general, none too fond of
Ortega because of his free-thinking forays. As an example of this, here are the following remarks of the
Dominican priest Guillermo Fraile, published in 1933,
on Ortega's merits as a literary artist:

A literary man? Beyond a doubt! How often do we encounter in his pages the beautiful and fresh and never-
before-spoken phrase, the perfect and delightful metaphor!
The freshly coined, still shiny adjective, sparkling, or with
the vigorous scent of fresh-cut wood! His pure prose flows
melodiously along with natural ease, ideas interweave and
disengage again without noise or haste, like curling cigarette
smoke. This prose is so fully "all twentieth century, and not
just modern" that it would seem at times that the ideas
themselves had chosen the words to fit them. Ortega gets
hold of a thought, hugs and caresses it, takes his deliberate
delight and pleasure in it. But he treats it with such affection that it never loses the charm of novelty. Whether he
turns to it just once, or twenty times, he can always be sure
that the idea has not lost its freshness and its charm. Ortega
possesses the art of dealing with a theme without destroying
it. He turns the luminous radiance of his masterful style

upon it, and all its parts are bathed in light. He does not need to reduce the whole into a pile of dust slipping from man's grasp. Ortega's reader always receives the pleasant sensation of consummate skill. Ortega writes effortlessly. He is like a lovely bird on the wing, whom we follow with our eyes until he is lost from sight. He starts his conversation in the middle range and never raises or lowers his voice, to the end. . . .

There are also these remarks, published in a journal in 1942, by Father Felix García. Among all Spanish priests he was probably closest to Ortega, whose family he was a friend of:

Ortega is the most resourceful rhetorician, the most adroit artist of literary style in all of Spain and Latin America. His prose is iridescent with the colors of the rainbow, and rings with wonderful music; at times it approaches absolute perfection. His images, metaphors, and turns of phrase, whether of his own coinage or borrowed, have achieved general currency and acceptance. His formulations and expressions have their own unmistakable elegance, which is infectious. On the other hand, we may occasionally catch him with ideas and idiosyncrasies that have no claim to being models of good taste. Ortega has the special art of enchanting us with his wisdom. It is not easy to resist the seductiveness of his Orphic prose with its melodious allurement. . . .

In *Imparcial,* Ortega published articles on the political situation that attracted nationwide attention by their sharp criticism of the politically maneuvering Spanish generals. The result of this Spanish self-examination was the birth of still another liberal newspaper, *El Sol.* It soon became the best among them, and for decades it was to be Ortega's favorite platform. His first series of articles, in 1920, in *El Sol,* on "The Liberation of the Provinces" ("La Rendición de las provincias") later became the first chapter of

*Invertebrate Spain (España invertebrada)*. This was his sharpest criticism of Spain, his most passionate but unhistorical and therefore most controversial book. (It was reprinted twice in the year of its publication, 1922). Though its style was admired by many, a still greater number of Spaniards regretted that it was translated into foreign languages. "This is the gloomiest book about Spain ever written," said Jiménez Caballero. Ortega himself was not comfortable about this scholarly lapse, and the book's almost embarrassing success made him feel insecure about his "attempt at an attempt to present ideas in highly concentrated, almost stenographic form." The fact is that Ortega the brilliant journalist had simply run away with Ortega the industrious amateur historian. In *Invertebrate Spain,* Ortega was mistaken in his representation of Gothic decadence in Spain, and was just as mistaken about the sociological consequences of Spain's Gothic past.

*4*

○○○○○○○○○○○○○○○○○○○○○○○○○○○○○○○○○○○○○○○○○○○○○○○

*Ortega*

*the*

*Ratiovitalist*

Whatever the defects of *Invertebrate Spain,* they were more than made up for by a series of books edited by Ortega from 1922 on and published as The Library of Twentieth-Century Ideas by Spain's leading publishers, Espasa-Calpe. These books introduced to Spain the principal works of Georg Wilhelm Friedrich Hegel, Edmund Husserl, and Oswald Spengler in translation; their influence made itself felt quickly. In 1922 Sigmund Freud's works in translation, with a warmly appreciative introduction by Ortega, were published. By 1927, however, he had somewhat cooled toward Freud. "I would almost take strong exception to Freud, if it were not, however, that . . . ," he hedged.

In 1923, Ortega rendered Spain an even greater service by founding the monthly *Revista de Occidente.* The great German critic E. R. Curtius, perhaps a little overenthusiastically, ranked it with the *Nouvelle Revue Française,* the *Neue Rundschau,* and *Criterion.* Whatever the Library of Ideas could not accomplish was left to the *Revista,* which proved extraordinarily fruitful during the years 1923 to 1936, in which it appeared. The *Revista* also absorbed Ortega's one-man journal, *El Espectador.* Ortega founded his own publishing house. (It continues to this day under the direction of his two sons, Miguel and José. Its well-designed paperbacks, moderately priced, enjoy the highest reputation in Spain and Latin America.)

The Library of Twentieth-Century Ideas was followed by a number of other series that comprised four hundred volumes. About seventy-five percent of these books were translations of German philosophical and historical works. Translations from the German of specialized studies in the fields of biology, ethnology, psychology, and economics were also offered to Spain and from there made their way to Latin America. Ortega surely was justified when he claimed proudly that he had repaid with interest his great debt to German learning by making it known throughout Spain and across the ocean, as its commentator, teacher, and publisher. Around the *Revista* Ortega assembled a group of translators not unlike the famous twelfth-century College of Translators of Toledo. He enlisted the best minds to make German and English authors (among whom were Franz Kafka, Aldous Huxley, and D. H. Lawrence) known throughout Spain. From 1910 on, he took it as his task to present to his countrymen the works of Europe's foremost thinkers. Drawing most heavily from among the ranks of German intellectuals, he contributed to the dissemination of the works of Wilhelm Worringer, Carl Jung, Sigmund Freud, Edmund Husserl, Max Scheler, Jakob Johann Üxküll, Hans Driesch, Georg Simmel, Werner Sombart, while his own striving for a personal philosophy found a haven with Martin Heidegger and Wilhelm Dilthey.

How deeply Ortega had penetrated into the center of German philosophy is amply documented by the fact that it was he who had to bring the work of the neglected philosopher Franz von Brentano to the attention of Hermann Cohen and, in 1923, of Albert Einstein. Ortega's own thinking was becoming noticeably freer and more original. His vitality and instinct for reality kept him from resting content with Hegel's primacy of the idea, or with Kant's primacy of practical reason, or with the primacy of culture of the neo-Kantians Hermann Cohen, Wilhelm Windelband, and Heinrich Rickert. What he found lacking in all the German "utopists" was an integrated and enduring sense of life joined with and purifying reason. In his set, being the most European mind in Spain, must have felt that the garrulous atmosphere of a Madrid café was unsuited to calm deliberations, and so the *tertulia* migrated to the editorial offices of the review and now meets in a round room hung with grey curtains and illuminated by discreet lamps. The migration has changed the meeting from a *tertulia* into a *cénacle*, or, to be more precise, a symposium, in which Ortega y Gasset plays the part of Socrates. I was intensely interested in the *tertulia* of this Spanish Socrates, because he has succeeded in doing for modern Spain what George Russell (AE) valiantly tried to do for modern Ireland with the *Irish Statesman*. Ortega y Gasset, like the bearded philosopher AE has the great range of mind and the wide sympathy that attracts the young idealists as well as the old. . . . The *Revista de Occidente* has made the voices of thinkers such as Einstein, Spengler, Keyserling heard in Spain. It has welcomed Paul Valéry, Marcel Proust, James Joyce. The room with the grey curtains is perched in a watch-tower high above the dust and conflict of Madrid, where not a whiff of Grub Street poisons the clear air. Around the squat, thickset little man with the leonine head I see historians and philosophers as well as men of letters. The conversation may pass from the Decline of the West to Belmonte the *Torero*; from *Los Borrachos* of Velázquez to Picasso's latest manner; from a violent speech in the *Cortes* by Largo Caballero, the Spanish Lenin, to the question whether *serenos* or night-watchmen are a relic of feudalism; but always the Master will draw together the scattered threads of the discourse and try to consider it *sub specie aeternitatis*.

To Ortega, his famous *tertulia* was one of the three focal points of his life; the other two were his teaching and his family. The *tertulia* would take up two to three hours of his time, every day of his life to the very end. The man who was being called *maestro* at the age of twenty-five is reported to have said that he would wish to die surrounded by this circle of friends; shortly before his death he talked lightly with them about his impending operation.

The mid-1920s were a fruitful period for Ortega the philosopher, whose writings grew richer in substance as his philosophical technique, became more ambitious. It was also an exciting period for Ortega the political man.

In 1923, with the consent of Alfonso XIII, General Miguel Primo de Rivera became chief of state of Spain at the head of a military directory. Ortega did not at first oppose this move because, like many intellectuals, he was disappointed in the party rule in the legislature with its resultant corruption. He was willing for power to be made available to one man because he believed that reform of the inner structure of Spain was more urgent than the establishment of a democracy. This attitude was reflected as late as 1927 and 1928 in the articles "The Surrender of the Provinces" ("La rendición de las provincias"), in which he stressed the necessity of regional reforms. But de Rivera proved to be a dilettantish patriarch who could not bring Spain out of its political stagnation. Thus, toward the end of the decade, when de Rivera wished to impose censorship, Ortega took his stand against him. This opposition has earned Ortega the reproach that he had failed to recognize a fateful moment in Spain's history when he refused to support de Rivera, a sound, constructive, high-minded statesman.

A fateful moment may have been missed in 1927 and 1928, when the leaders of Spain's Catholic renascence failed to make common cause with Ortega, who at that time was closer to them than at any other time in his eventful life. By temperament an optimist, fundamentally a stoic (as a Spaniard), a master of the art of living and of shaping men's minds, Ortega knew how to parry life's adversities with a smile. He was not a man to let others look deeply into his heart. He was generally reticent about his attitude toward God. Only this much he has told us: that every morning he sent heavenward an ancient Indian prayer, "Lord, let us wake up cheerfully, and grant us understanding!"

But there are three essays from the year 1927 that reveal him, ardent an antimetaphysician as he was, as exceptionally open-minded on religious questions: "God in Sight" ("Dios a la vista"); the "Dialogue" concerning Henri Massis, in which he urged his countrymen to listen not to this Frenchman but to the more tolerant and irenic German writers on Catholicism, Romano Guardini, Erich Przywara, and Max Scheler; "Social Power" ("Poder social"), in which he enjoins the liberals to give up their obsolete anticlericalism. Ortega confessed that he had discovered his own "Catholic predisposition." According to Pedro Laín Entralgo, the medical historian and philosopher, a meeting of minds between Ortega and the most stable pillar of Spanish culture, the Catholic church, could probably have been fruitful at that time, with a little more understanding, generosity, and tolerance on both sides.

We are inclined to suspect that the growing political tension in Ortega's mind, as in that of Unamuno, prevented him from reaching the intellectual clarity that might have been decisive. Spain's inner discord thus lived on in the hearts of its intellectual elite. The fateful moments in a nation's history never recur in the same form. Spain's intellectual stagnation and metaphysical aridity dimmed Ortega's external triumphs in public and political life despite all his efforts.

In 1928, Ortega went once more to lecture in Argentina. At this time he avoided his estranged friend Maeztu, who was then, as one of de Rivera's men, an ambassador in Buenos Aires.

The opposition of the Spanish intelligentsia to de Rivera had grown sharper and more unyielding. A wave of protest against the exile of Miguel de Unamuno was sweeping the country. In 1929 Ortega himself, in an act of academic solidarity, resigned his teaching position at the Central University of Madrid.

In the spring of 1929, Ortega offered a series of ten lectures in Madrid's auditoriums, and once again won admiration from the nation's capital. Lofty, detached, lucid, and wholly free of political controversy, these lectures on the theme "What Is Philosophy?" (published after Ortega's death, in 1958) revealed his long-standing preference for Augustinian Christianity and his own ratiovitalism. Ortega proposed to renew his deeply troubled country by means of "integrity, clarity, and accuracy" at the very moment when Spain's social problems and political instability were crying out for drastic emergency action: Ortega was still the incorrigible dreamer of lofty dreams!

In the course of a decade, from *Meditations on Don Quixote* to *The Modern Theme* (1923) and *Neither Vitalism nor Rationalism* (1924), Ortega developed his theory of ratiovitalism. As he came to believe in these years, neither realism nor idealism, therefore neither Kant nor Hegel, came to grips with the true nature of human life—its "radical reality" (*realidad radical*). Because the "I" exists only in his physical and cultural environment, he has to live in terms of it and has finally to master its facets. Ortega defined man with a formula that has become famous:

I am myself plus my circumstances (*Yo soy yo y mi circunstancia*). Above Kant's pure and scientific reason stands Ortega's ratiovitalism, which is "the one and the same thing as life itself." It is only the facets of life that give reason to man and his circumstances and make them comprehensible. And, since life takes place in history, reason can only occur in history, not as an abstract, disembodied entity that is extratemporal and extraspatial.

As a philosopher, Ortega had always been better at diagnosing ills than at building systems. Now again, he sensed the portents in the air. His most successful book, *The Revolt of the Masses* (*La rebelión de las masas*), appeared in August 1930. An international success, translated into ten languages, the book threatens to lead astray those who understand it as the sum total of Ortega's philosophy and classify him by it. The critics in the United States took the easy way out: they simply drew a straight line from Jean-Jacques Rousseau's *Social Contract,* through Karl Marx's *Capital,* to Ortega's *Revolt of the Masses,* omitting all the intervening links of the twentieth century, such as Oswald Spengler's *Decline of the West* and *Prussianism and Socialism* or Hermann Keyserling's *The Specter of Europe.* German social scientists today scoff at the unscientific character of what Spaniards have called his "most widely read and best written book."

But *The Revolt of the Masses* was, is, and will remain a standard work of European self-criticism and one of the earliest calls for European integration, a document championing a new kind of supranational fatherland that can still be useful to our own age that is so desperately lacking in models that could give us guidance. Europe, Ortega wrote, is to be established not as an "inter-nation" but as an "ultra-nation," one that would make its appeal to human reason and the human heart.

To make these essays, written for Spaniards, fully intelligible in other countries, Ortega added special introductions to the French and the English translations. The special introduction intended for the German edition of 1934 was not allowed to be published for political reasons (this was the year after Adolf Hitler came to power in Germany). It was not to be published until 1957 in German. Doubtless the enormously successful book contains some faulty scholarship. The word masses shifts from a value concept to a psychological concept, and in the end even becomes a moral standard. "Multitude" turns into a sociological community. The elite is praised highly but never defined. The work has lent itself to much misuse. On the left, Ortega's basic hierarchic-aristocratic attitude and his criticism of the lack of taste and culture among the masses of our era were simply disregraded. On the right, his criticism of aimless liberalism and of the democracies "in an age of universal blackmail" were read simplistically as an endorsement of reactionary thinking.

In his earliest pronouncements Ortega was already critical of "cloying liberalism," and it appears certain that in the 1920s he became ever more receptive to conservative ideas. He never shared Hegel's idolization of the state. In full agreement with the poet Juan Ramón Jiménez, his friend, Ortega demanded intellectual and moral freedom for the elite, the eminent minority (*immensa minoría*). Just as Hermann Hesse had scorned his era for the degeneration that he epitomized in his label "the age of the feuilleton," so Ortega attacked the "culture of verbiage" and the "reign of the shop window." These, along

And then came 1931 and the second republic, eagerly hoped for and prepared for by the majority of Spain's intellectuals, launched by Ortega's friends. In his own writings he was actively on the side of its establishment although he did not directly participate in bringing it into being. Indirectly, he may have precipitated the end of the lingering monarchy by branding General Berenguer as the scapegoat who must atone for the deadlocked system. The main function of Berenguer, the weak successor of Primo de Rivera, was to assist in the burial of the monarchy. In a strong article in *El Sol* of 15 November 1930, Ortega had pilloried the Spanish government as ruined and exhausted, and had closed with the call that marked a turning point in Spanish history: the monarchy must be destroyed (*delenda est monarchia!*). Five months later, that time had come.

King Alfonso XIII's regime was crumbling. Ortega and his friends Pérez de Ayala and Marañón, in a manifesto of 10 February 1931, had made an attempt to mobilize the intelligentsia of the nation in his new Asociación al Servicio de la República. But that group was far too sophisticated to gain ground as a popular party. The clergy, "respected members of society," had been invited, needless to say in vain, to join the group. In April, power passed into the hands of the second republic without friction, bloodshed, or coup d'état. It was a picture of fumbling and weakness. It was all a consequence of the overestimation of the importance of the county elections.

Ortega greeted the "republic of simplicity and plain talk." In June he allowed himself to be elected to the legislature as delegate of the province of León (his term of office was 1931 to 1933). Thirteen of his friends were also elected. But being only fourteen strong in a legislative body of four hundred fifty-seven delegates, among whom one hundred forty-nine were freemasons, meant they were only a minuscule, isolated progressive party, whose influence was purely oratorical. This group suffered from one basic defect, which, after one and a half years, brought about its demise. As Ortega himself had repeatedly noted (once, for instance, at a meeting in Segovia in February 1931), the members of this circle looked upon themselves as intellectuals and public benefactors, not as managers of power and career politicians. They made greater demands on themselves and on their fellow members than did the other delegates, but, lacking the stamina for democratic compromise, they were no match for the powerful political instincts and skilled trickery of functionaries and officials. Ultimately they were no more than the pitiful victims of noble self-deception, a fact that had been obvious from the start.

Ortega himself declined many opportunities to seriously enter political life. The presidency, the ministry of foreign affairs, the post of ambassador to Berlin—all three were within his grasp. Instead, returning to his teaching position at the Central University of Madrid, he devoted himself to the renewal and improvement of the university and offered counsel, and at times unsolicited instruction, to the politicians. "But his new pupils did not understand him," wrote Joaquín Arrarás in *The History of the Second Spanish Republic* (1956). His language was too lofty and too learned for the delegates' taste. Neither the working classes nor the party functionaries were prepared to accept his claim (made on 31 July 1931) that "he, too, was a working man who had sacrificed his life and health to daily toil."

Even during his incumbency in the legislature,

Ortega maintained his personal style, his independent way of thinking, and his aestheticism, although he often had to fight for it: "I don't mean to pretend being what I am not. A literary man, a thinker, a theoretician, a friend of science—all this I do not just pretend to be. Why the devil, that is exactly what I am, down to the marrow!" Just as his fellow academicians who were merely specialists disliked his many-sidedness, those men who were only politicians disliked his intellectual superiority. In our century, the century of the specialist, it is simply not enough to be a nonspecialist and act accordingly; however vast a nonspecialist's knowledge may be, his efforts will end in tragedy. Ortega is the living proof.

Ortega's life during the years of the second republic is probably its most interesting, most controversial, and darkest chapter. We can shed little light on it, because Ortega himself is of no help here. Only the basic outlines of that period can be discerned by the aid of his lectures and the pronouncements of his friends and foes.

Ortega's life can serve as an example of the intellectual's fate in the twentieth century. For five decades Spain's left-wing intellectuals had waited for the establishment of the republic. In five short years the republic was bankrupt. As Fuentes Rojo wrote, the republic "had shown itself incapable of solving a single one of Spain's many social and political, economic and cultural problems—on the contrary, the republic had only complicated all these problems." Years later Ortega would still express his distress at "those demagogues, those impresarios of self-alienation."

But Ortega himself was often mistaken in his appraisals of the various stages in the republic's decline. In August 1931, he called the new constitution "simply splendid," declared that a second chamber, one designed to exert a conservative and stabilizing function, was superfluous, and regarded the separation of church and state—an unheard-of matter in Spain—as a *fait accompli*. One year later he fully agreed with Madariaga, Unamuno, and Alejandro Lerroux, the liberal, anticlerical politican, rejecting "this sorry constitution that has neither head nor feet, and what there is between head and feet is also not organic." As for his own role in the legislature he declined "to play the clown, the tenor, or the wild boar."

Pío Baroja y Nessi, his highly critical friend, said of the idealistic and indeed utopian politician Ortega: "Where others drown, he swims." Ortega had utterly miscalculated the objectives and the educability of the workers, the share of the provinces in the life of the federal state, and the working capacity of Spain's legislature, all of which are mistakes that do him honor as a philosopher and humanist. The most important political interlude in Ortega's life began with skeptical witticisms, continued with protests, and ended in despair and alienation. In April, the very month when the Spanish second republic was born, he could still say: "Almost everything that is interesting in Spanish history has come from the prison cell—Don Quixote and the republic." Spain, he could then claim, needed nothing from abroad: "Spain will succeed on her own!" (*España fará de se!*). One month later, he warned that the educated must caution the working classes against further excesses, such as the burning of churches and monasteries, which the government was then tolerating.

In addition, Ortega felt that the elections had not been conducted with decency and fairness: "Untalented adventurers without morals, political under-

standing, or spirit" had moved into the legislature, in
which Ortega was raising his voice in vain against re-
venge and radicalism, calling for cooperation among
the social classes and among the provinces, and em-
phasizing, above all, the need for economic planning.
Before the republic was six months old, Ortega cried:
"This is not what we wanted!" His phrase *Eso no es!*
has entered into the Spanish language.

Manuel Azaña y Diez, Ortega's old enemy who
had meanwhile risen from unsuccessful writer to prime
minister, came back with a strong reply and remained
in power unchallenged. Political decisions were being
made on the basis of political factions, not principles.

Ortega, republican without peer, who in this government of the masses represented the elite, and who
in vain sought to realize his ideals, made yet another
mighty effort to salvage the situation. His small team
had been keeping fairly quiet, and even their rare
speeches failed to influence their dull-witted colleagues
in the legislature. Ortega, leader of the group, finally
took the floor himself, on 6 December 1931, with an
important public speech in one of Madrid's largest
motion picture theaters. He called for an end to "this
sad republic gone sour," to the weak ministries, to the
general embitterment; he called for a new centrist
party under the leadership of the moderate conservative Miguel Maura. It was all in vain. Ortega's final
plan of reform failed, just as his youthful first attempt
of 1914 had failed.

By the time the second republic was one year old,
the great novelist Pío Baroja y Nessi had turned his
back on it. ("No one has faith in the constitution," he
wrote on 5 February 1932.) So had the honored citizen
of the nation who had returned from exile, Miguel de

Unamuno. ("The Inquisition had certain guarantees. Today's police inquisition is far worse; it is based on collective panic, it invents dangers in order to secure emergency legislation." This was his comment on 28 November 1932.)

Ortega still took an active part in the legislative struggles over the settlement of the long-standing problem of autonomy for Catalonia. Being a Castilian, he argued strongly in favor of centralism, a position that led to frequent clashes with Prime Minister Azaña. These two liberal republicans, both pillars of the new government, became such violent enemies that the prime minister could lump Ortega with disgruntled generals and conservative monarchists under the one epithet "gravediggers of the republic!" Spain's two finest minds, Ortega and Unamuno, buried their differences to join forces against the opportunistic power politicians.

The aged Miguel de Unamuno even attempted to draw down upon himself another persecution by the government, another exile. In November 1932, Ortega disbanded his little group: the spirit had capitulated in the face of power politics. José Gaos, Ortega's finest former student, then dean of the Central University of Madrid, who had joined the Spanish socialists years earlier, would later accuse Ortega of impatience in political matters, and thus indirectly blame him for the failure of the second republic.

To make a point, we may cite Alfred Weber, cofounder of Germany's Democratic Party in the Weimar Republic, speaking of his own parallel case: "By the end of 1918, it was already clear to me that I was out of place here among these hardboiled political professionals with their cast-iron nerves. I returned to Heidelberg and resumed my teaching, and my scholarly researches." So did Ortega.

Or again, there is Karl Jaspers's comment about the great sociologist (a brother of Alfred Weber) Max Weber, his teacher whom he revered: "Was he a scholar or a politician? He was a patriot. Neither politics nor scholarship were of central, sole, absolute importance to him. . . . The guiding idea of his philosophical existence is in the last analysis a mystery, as are all great things."

Ortega the "political failure" no doubt had the French poet Alfred de Musset's remark in mind that "politics is like a delicate spider web, with many miserable crippled flies twitching in it." In fact, Ortega himself almost became such a fly in the days to come, when the second republic of Spain was to end in bloodshed. He grew more thoughtful now, reminded himself of history and its hidden laws, and turned his mind's eye still more steadily toward Europe. Abroad, his articles and essays were being collected in book form, and his fame grew daily. The first edition of his collected works (1946) opened with the proud and skeptical statement: "My entire work and my whole life have been in the service of Spain. This is an incontestable truth, though on the whole and seen objectively, it leads up to the fact that nothing came of it." Nonetheless he believed firmly that "the Spanish spirit has been saved."

At home and abroad, Ortega kept repeating his warnings against "a relapse into barbarism." He, like Unamuno, foresaw the coming of the Spanish civil war. The two men started to see each other again in the *tertulia* of the *Revista de Occidente,* but the younger host courteously steered clear of the older guest. In temperament, they were too different. In the thinking of both, Spain's national tradition and internal equilibrium loomed larger now. In 1933, Ortega urged in a radio speech: "We must allow our time to take its time, we must wait and wait until we achieve clarity about man's future." A man of the radical center, he warned against extremism of both the left and the right, seeing as dangerous both the communism and fascism rising all over Europe. He demanded: "Look into yourselves!" And he expressed his belief that "almost all of Spain's youth" was hanging on his lips.

In the summer of 1933, in the international lecture series at Santander, Ortega, sharing the platform with the philosophers Manuel García Morente and Xavier Zubiri, delivered a series of lectures on technology. Karl Vossler mentioned the event to his friend, the Italian philosopher Benedetto Croce, as "a great oratorical success." It was surely a moral success for Ortega that in this same year he had the opportunity to help Angel Herrera, editor of Madrid's Catholic journal *El Debate,* in his desperate struggles with the government.

Those were the final years of Ortega's splendor as a teacher, when his mind turned once more toward his true profession. Did he do so for lack of a better commitment? Or did he return because he now felt he had a more profound understanding of many matters?

On 18 November 1955, Gregorio Marañón was to eulogize his dead friend, in the address *In Memoriam: Professor Don José Ortega y Gasset,* as Ortega the teacher *(maestro)* and rate him much higher than Ortega the academician *(catedrático)* or Ortega the educational administrator. (This address, which ran to seventy-seven pages, was published as a monograph by the University of Madrid in 1955.)

Ortega taught his subject, but, like all great teachers, taught much else besides. His work on the university, for example, through the medium of the *Revista de Occidente* is perhaps one of the most effective performances of recent years anywhere within the echelons of Spain's higher education. . . . The informal conversations at night in the editorial office of the *Revista* had a truly academic character in their conversational technique, and conversation, as we know, is indeed the best way to teach. How many of my colleagues have I since then heard bemoaning the fact that we possess no written records to preserve for us the spontaneous remarks he made during those hours! There were impromptu speeches that had all the marks of a rigorously structured lecture; there were comments that consisted of a sentence or so tossed into a conversation, and yet they were worth a whole hour of lecturing. It matters little that they have not been recorded. They will endure, as furrows cut by Ortega's words into our minds, and sooner or later they will yield their harvest. Many of Ortega's students are no longer certain today whether they heard him speak his thoughts from the lectern, or read them in his books, or whether these thoughts flashed pyrotechnically from the pages of the *Revista,* or whether they came from conversations they had with the master on their travels with him. For Ortega was a great teacher always, and gave lavishly of his knowledge and his wisdom even when he had but a single listener.

Although Ortega was not to return to Germany until 1934, his fame had spread throughout that country ever since an enterprising German publisher, Kilpper, had come upon the scene. Kilpper "became excited to the point of enthusiasm" at first reading Ortega's writings; he became Ortega's principal publisher, while E. R. Curtius and Helene Weyl introduced "the German" Ortega to the public at large. It should be noted here that in Germany, just as in

France and in Argentina, women have contributed a major share to the success of this philosopher who was so elegant in person and in style that his Spanish critic Vincente Marrero called him the prototype of "urbanity." Ortega expressed gratitude to Kilpper with characteristic Spanish *exageración*: without Kilpper, he said, he would have remained "an unknown philosophy professor in Madrid." This is hardly an accurate statement, considering his fame in South America alone.

That same year, 1934, Ortega wrote for the first time a full account of his thought specifically intended for a German audience, a personal dialogue with his "intellectual fathers," *A Prologue for Germans (Prólogo para alemanes)*. He acknowledged his great debt to them, but also presented a counterclaim: his own share in spreading German thought throughout Spain and especially through South America. In sum, he said, "we are even"—which, as I see it, is true. The essay, which runs to seventy pages in the Spanish publication, also offers a very readable history of German philosophy from Kant to Husserl and culminates in a declaration of love for Wilhelm Dilthey.

*The Revolt of the Masses* remained a best seller in Germany (300,000 copies have been sold by now) regardless of political regime because all factions found in its pages something of value to them. Ortega now became a steady contributor, indeed almost a staff member, of the Stuttgart journal *Europäische Revue.* The editor of that journal, Joachim Moras, denies that Germany's Third Reich was sealed off from intellectual life abroad; the isolation, he declared, had been selective. "We could read T. S. Eliot, Paul Valéry, and André Gide, but not W. H. Auden or André Malraux. We did have Pío Baroja y Nessi and Gomez de

la Serna, and again and again Ortega, but no García
Lorca."

In 1935, in Buenos Aires, Ortega published five
substantial essays of his impressions of his travels in
Germany; they steered clear of politics. Had he drawn
a lesson from his experiences in the Madrid legislature, and vowed to abstain from politics? There is not
one critical word about National Socialism, only
words of admiration "for the extraordinary results
. . . the gigantic attempt. . . ." In the first draft of
the essay "Man and People," one critical sentence was
devoted to the wave of killings Hitler unleashed in the
Röhm affair of 1934, but that sentence was struck out.
It said that this episode had prompted Ortega to withdraw by telegram his permission to publish his *Prologue for Germans* in Germany. (In 1934, Hitler ar-
rested Ernst Röhm, who was head of the Nazi Party's
SA, on the charge that he was intriguing to overthrow
Hitler. Subsequently he unleashed a reign of terror
against the members of Röhm's faction, and a savage
massacre was carried out in the name of defending the
country against traitors.)

It was as though Ortega's power of language had
become confused, and so he held back and waited, unable to foresee what the "masses," in Spain, in Italy,
and in Germany, would yet have to offer or to suffer.
Could he who had been so grossly mistaken about his
own country now take on the role of prophet for all
Europe? When his friends, in 1934, joined in public
demonstrations in support of former Prime Minister
Azaña, Ortega kept aloof. Was his new position to be
that "politics is a dirty game"? He was not idle, however; to his German publisher, he wrote: "A man has
to be and do many things at the same time: writer,
politician, café conversationalist, bullfighter. These

last three years (1931 to 1934) have been especially disastrous for me." His correspondence with his German friends became irregular.

A proud man, Ortega avoided public honors as a matter of principle. He refused to accept the Order of the Republic offered to him in 1935 on the occasion of his twenty-fifth anniversary as professor at the Central University of Madrid. But in December of the same year, when Madrid's city council (of which his brother Eduardo was a member) elected him unanimously by secret ballot to receive the gold medal of Madrid, Ortega could not refuse to accept this homage transcending all party lines and offered to him by his native city. The day on which he received it also brought him a very sharp reproof. It came from his most brilliant and most devoted pupil, José Antonio Primo de Rivera, son of the late dictator, a lawyer who, because of Ortega's recent political inertia, had become the founder of the Falangist party. Traditionalist opponents regarded this first Spanish fascist leader as "a second-rate Ortega" (the phrase was coined by Elías de Tejada) and an ideologue who stepped forward when Ortega refused to face harsh reality. On 29 October 1933, one year after Ortega's political retirement, that party that stood for hierarchical revolution (as opposed to anarchic revolution), national reform, and control of the masses by an elite of conviction was founded at the Teatro de la Comedia—the very place where Ortega, twenty years earlier, had made his vain attempt to enter practical politics.

Was it coincidental only that the Teatro de la Comedia was chosen as the place for the founding of the new party? As late as 1935 Rivera was still hoping to secure the official approval of his much admired preceptor. Ortega's support would by then be all the

more desirable and useful because the other venerable
patriarch, Unamuno, had shunned Rivera's invitation,
and withdrawn into the solitude of embittered resigna-
tion. Ortega, too, rejected Rivera's overtures, and thus
Rivera's veneration changed into the reproach: "Leaders have no right to withdraw!" The young Rivera
was convinced that Ortega's exceptional qualifications,
"acumen, integrity, and objectivity," imposed on him
the duty of continuing to take an active part in
politics.

But Ortega remained aloof, despite the fact that
many of his young friends and even his own sons
joined the Falangist party, which, young as it was, was
engendering the most activity in the nation. In its
terminology and many of its catchphrases, it was an
expression of Ortega's spirit. There is good reason,
then, to count him among the seedbearers of revolution, along with Rousseau, Marx, and Nietzsche,
though in this instance, and in others still to come,
the fruit bore little resemblance to the seeds he had
planted.

It is also true that such a leading socialist as José
Gaos, dean of the Central University of Madrid during the time of the second republic, was a former student of Ortega. (Gaos died in 1969, an expatriate in
Mexico.) The fact is that Ortega, in politics as in philosophy, tended to stimulate minds rather than give
people a firm road to follow. But there is little doubt
that the aristocratic *falange* (literally, phalanx) was
closer to Ortega's temperament than the socialism of
the proletarians, a love of his youth he had jilted long
ago. What possible use could the radical Spanish left
make of the rueful confession he admitted during
these years. "We felt the spirit of the times but not

that of the past, because we did not know the past!"
On the very eve of the fratricidal civil war, Ortega did
have an intimation that Spain needed a fundamental
change: "The Spaniard," he said, "must convert!" But
the trouble was that he did not know how that *con-
versión* was to come about; he was unable to point the
way even to his own students. For years he had, in a
sense, expatriated himself, though living in the heart
of Spain.

In 1936, when the internal struggles within the
left erupted, the radicals and usurpers considered Ortega an embarrassment. Along with other leading intellectuals, he was coerced into publicly supporting the
struggling but hollow republic of the left. It reached
the point where Ortega, now seriously ill, was no
longer safe from attempts on his life. With French
help he escaped in 1936 to France, where he would
soon have to face dangerous surgery. Once in exile, he
openly broke with the leftist republicans; his sons
joined Franco's forces.

In Paris, convalescing and in economic straits, Ortega had ample leisure to realize how right Maeztu had
been—Maeztu, one of the earliest victims of the chaos,
had met a violent death in a Madrid prison in November 1936. For even while the socialists were attacking Ortega as a petit bourgeois, Maeztu, in one of his
last articles (dated 20 April 1936) had pilloried Ortega
as an amoral relativist and ideological opportunist
who, without meaning to, had served as the trailblazer
of the revolution: "He is much too fond of adapting
his thinking to whatever situation prevails at the moment of his writing."

The men who in 1931 had overthrown King Alfonso XIII—Ortega, Marañón, Pérez de Ayala—had

now themselves been overthrown and had followed the king into exile. The *action directe* of the "revolt of the masses" was in full swing.

The Netherlands offered brief refuge to Ortega. While there, he wrote a few short contributions for *La Nación* of Buenos Aires. Among them was an essay on Dutch bicycles! A short foreword he wrote for the French edition of *The Revolt of the Masses,* was brilliant, witty, urbane as ever, for a true *caballero* keeps his composure even in distress. When Unamuno, his fellow fighter and rival, died on 31 December 1936, rejected by both the left-wingers and the reactionaries, Ortega joined Spain in the mourning. In the obituary Ortega wrote, however, he did not fail to mention his differences with Unamuno: "We philosophers are not amateurs, we are craftsmen," he wrote. Unamuno, however, as a true '98er, belonged among the romantics and noble dilettantes of the mind, a member of the generation of that other utopian, George Bernard Shaw.

The Spanish civil war claimed a million lives before it finally came to an end in March 1939. One month after it was over, Ortega from abroad sent a warning to his young friend Marías that he must try to "recover equanimity, that great Spanish composure, the classic Spanish gesture that foreigners so often speak of as our 'Spanish gravity.'" Only this composure could serve as the foundation on which the lives of the citizenry and the community could be rebuilt. This battle-scarred and still incorrigibly optimistic man—does he not deserve our admiration?

Ortega did not return to Spain at once. Not yet. From 1939 to 1942, he remained in Argentina, reaping new triumphs. But even this third sojourn in South America, a rather uneventful one, did not prompt Ortega to make his home by the Rio de la Plata. The new world was to him an interesting experience, but not the native soil on which a European of Spanish blood could thrive.

Ortega, who never liked to talk about himself, felt entitled now to address his critics from beyond the Atlantic: "For five years now I have been wandering all over the world, homeless. I have gone from one country to another, one continent to another. I have known every misfortune, and have suffered sickness that has brought me to the brink of death."

As early as 1940, Ortega had been elected in absentia to membership in Spain's highest cultural academy, the Consejo de la Hispanidad. He never, however, took an active part in it. In 1942, with his wife and daughter, he went to live in the south of Portugal. It was the year in which he wrote to his friend Marías that "the hour calls for action, action, and more action!"

Pressed for money, Ortega became the editor of

the publishing firm Azar, for which he planned the series "Knowing Man." In 1944, he moved to Estoril, a luxurious seaside resort near Lisbon. In that year he paid a short visit to his native Spain. In 1945 he returned to Madrid for a short stay. The homecoming of Spain's most famous citizen, at a time when Spain was excluded from the United Nations, meant great moral support and was gratefully received as such by his countrymen.

Ortega stayed in Madrid only briefly. The old favorite vacation resort, the shell-strewn bay of San Sebastián, fashionable yet lovely, claimed him once more. He sought the hospitality of the inn at Zumaya, as he had done a dozen times in the past. This world traveler, now home again, invariably came back to his old haunts. Madrid, that beloved, elegant, and lively city, drew him more strongly now than ever before. Yet four more years were to pass before he and his family could fully adapt themselves to the radically changed conditions and resettle permanently in Madrid.

Ortega once confessed to Keyserling, his closest German friend, that "he simply could not for long live away from Madrid, where all knew him and he knew all." He liked to think of himself as an aristocratic "philosopher in the marketplace." And the alluring, easy-going city of Madrid was the magnet that attracted him so strongly that he put aside even his political reservations.

Ortega and Franco, chief of state after the Spanish civil war, never met. They were equally proud men. This bitter fact, too, is significant. In any case, Ortega's response was generous and high-spirited: "The government pays no attention whatever to me, nor does it meddle in my affairs." This remark was not altogether true of the government's censors, who did not look with unalloyed pleasure at Ortega's popularity or at the public triumphs of this man who had returned from exile only provisionally and conditionally. They made no secret of their displeasure.

Ortega, as if rejuvenated by his return to his homeland, was exuberant with creative energy and intellectual vitality. His lectures on Leibniz's Optimism, delivered at Madrid and in San Sebastián, launched his last great campaign for an intellectually integrated Europe. Leibniz, he proposed, was Europe's last polyhistor. After him came that philosophical pessimism against which he, Ortega, son of the sunny south, had battled all his life. His lectures were well received by scholars and the nobility alike (among the latter, the powerful Count Alba was Ortega's personal friend). This success, together with his ardent faith in the youth of Spain, prompted Ortega, who held a professorial post in name only, to forcibly harmonize the public interest and his personal financial needs.

In the winter semester 1948 to 1949, the Instituto de Humanidades opened in Madrid. It was an important private center for lectures provided mainly by Ortega and Marías. Ortega, the founder, offered as the principal lecture course a series analyzing, and favorably commenting on, Arnold Toynbee's philosophy of history. The Old Testament, the history of the Roman Empire, the changing fortunes of Spain's history—they all provided Ortega with occasions and examples in which he could drive home his own point of view and address his praises or reproofs, disguised but unmistakable, to Franco. At that fateful hour in Spanish history, it was both proper and desirable for Ortega to explain, by simile and metaphor, how a new legal state may arise out of an illegal act, how Franco might yet become Spain's Augustus. It seems strange that no close ties developed between Franco and Ortega. Even Ortega's appeal to the students—"Young fellows, there are many things we must talk over together!"—seems to have fallen on deaf ears.

Some of the critical young Falangists accused Ortega of being unable to cast aside his obsolete thinking. Others regarded the repatriated Ortega a prisoner of his own ideas, incapable of new conceptions. He was, in the words of García Escudero, a monument that "only death will render human again." In a second lecture series, delivered in 1949 and 1950, Ortega treated his Madrid audiences to his own unorthodox, stimulating, and at times wayward brand of sociology, his theory of "men and people." But the response to him remained the same: he continued to be isolated, though eminent, and the reaction he craved so much stayed uncertain and confused. Small wonder, then, that he escaped more and more often to the soil from which he drew his intellectual sustenance, the lands in which he found a much broader response: Europe north of the Pyrenees.

Now came Ortega's third, and last, meeting with the German intelligentsia. His full absorption into the intellectual mainstream of West Germany, his lasting friendships with Germany's best minds, began in these years. The celebrations in honor of the two-hundredth anniversary of Goethe's birth, in 1949, provided the occasion for Ortega to do this.

The tide of festivities, memorial celebrations, and special radio programs that marked the event was given a new face by the presence of such men as Theodor Heuss, President of the German Federal Republic, and José Ortega y Gasset. In 1951, Heuss was to recall that "the nation's demand, if I may say so, for speeches about Goethe was adequately fulfilled in 1949." If the truth is to be told, Ortega contributed his share to the abundance of Goethe speeches. He had come to Germany, his intellectual home, his second country, burdened perhaps by a need to compensate for his recent experience in Spain, but once there he was infused with new energy inspired by the return to the scenes of his youth and moved by the enthusiasm of a man who was committed to rebuilding and reforming Spain and Europe. Anyone who has ever turned the pages of Ortega's controversial *A Plea to Look at the Inner Goethe (Pidiendo un Goethe desde dentro),* his commemorative book in 1932, on the hundredth anniversary of Goethe's death, will have recognized that these are the words of a man who spoke of Germany's greatest man with certain reservations, though with profound respect and understanding.

In 1949 Ortega was invited to the United States, to speak on Goethe before a large international audience at Aspen, Colorado. His first and last visit to the northern half of the new world compelled him, incidentally, to revise his prejudices, and henceforth to look with more respect at the English-speaking people beyond the ocean. In New York City, the visitor received the highest honors from the Hispanic Society and met again his dear old German friend, the world-renowned scholar E. R. Curtius.

The crowning event of the latter part of Ortega's public life was, however, surely his homecoming to the new Germany. His reception was triumphal. In Hamburg, the university's largest auditorium was packed with students, professors, and dignitaries, who waited patiently for an hour while Ortega went to get the notes he had forgotten at the hotel. Ortega even visited a fashion show, allowing himself to be interviewed on that occasion. His visits in northern Germany were followed by lectures in Düsseldorf, Berlin, Stuttgart, and Frankfurt; this last city honored the Spanish speaker with its Goethe medal. (Ortega's Goethe lectures, in which he never repeated himself, are still awaiting publication.) Many a German newspaper reader may have groaned in 1949: "Ortega again. When will it ever end?"

West Germany's leading newspaper of that time, the *Neue Zeitung,* celebrated Christmas of 1949 with a full page on Ortega's private academy in Madrid, asserting it was an institution that would be the prototype of a new "University of Life." Six years later, after Ortega died, Spain's leading art historian, Lafuente Ferrari, was still clamoring for Ortega's lofty and profound plan to be made at last a living reality. To this day, Ferrari's demand has not been met.

The platform in West Germany of greatest interest to Ortega was doubtless the one provided by the Darmstadt Colloquia, a round table of outstanding thinkers in which he joined several times. It was the same platform on which his friend Keyserling, in the fruitful and restless 1930s, had offered a living example of his universal dream of a "School of Wisdom," leaving a challenging legacy to the city of Darmstadt. The colloquium of 1951 dealt with "Man and Space," with man's building and dwelling on earth, and with the ethos of rebuilding the war-ravaged German towns, a situation that, Ortega believed, offered the Germans an opportunity to make a wholly new creative start.

Perhaps it was a high point, even *the* high point, in the life of Ortega when, on 5 August 1951, in Darmstadt's town hall, he met Martin Heidegger, crossed lances with him, and held his own. On the one side, Germany's solitary uncrowned philosopher-king propounded a doctrine of mystical wisdom. On the other, the popular and even more controversial philosopher-for-everyman from abroad, who had so often competed with Heidegger for recognition and independence, who had trumpeted his claim to intellectual priority in the daily press (convincingly if not always tastefully), raised his opposing voice.

That Sunday morning, Heidegger's "mortals must ever learn to dwell!" held the stage. But the afternoon belonged to Ortega, to whose "elegant intelligence" man seemed a being "sick in nature," "born dismayed" into the new world of technology, who tried to distract himself by a "gigantic orthopedic apparatus." Ortega provided his audience with thought and with laughter as he offered himself as a radically "dissecting thinker, such as the good Lord needs to keep all the other animals from falling asleep." The self-willed Ortega, inviting mankind once more to embrace life with all its demands, and challenging the illusory world of German theorizing, confused and delighted the astonished crowd. The direct attack on the still immature modern architecture, and the long overdue sideswipe at Heidegger's overly mysterious profundities, were left to Alfred Weber.

These were the days when Ortega found a new love in Germany, the city of Munich. There he made friends among the students and professors of the university. There he struck roots so deep that in September 1951 the *Abendzeitung* of Munich could report: "For the fifth time, the Spanish philosopher Ortega y Gasset visited the Oktoberfest and happily raised his stein in Schottenhamel's beer hall." Unrecognized by the crowd, Ortega quietly enjoyed the colorful spectacle of the festive masses milling under the noisy tent. The turbulent Bavarian festival does not seem to have shaken his convictions concerning the nature of man.

Not much later, still in October, Ortega once again confronted Heidegger, at a meeting in Bühlerhöhe. Heidegger here rejected both Nietzsche's view that man is "an animal that turned out wrong," and Ortega's view of man as "a contrite animal that mended its ways." Instead Heidegger placed man into the "unifying four of heaven and earth, gods and mortals."

In November, in Munich once more, we hear Ortega offer challenging wisdom to Germany's educators in a publication of the International Youth Library. It was a wisdom sprung from the soul of a man who knew, loved, and served youth, not a wisdom drawn from handbooks of pedagogy. While German educators were still contesting the right of the young to read the sometimes crude and often gory fairy tales and sagas, Ortega, even then a long step ahead of them, urged the young to steep themselves in mythology. He opposed "education for maturity" and instead championed a full, complete childhood, because "the best man is he who has been most fully a child." Ortega understood children, and the young in their turn liked him. There is today hardly a good high-school reader in Germany that does not include some pieces by Ortega, introducing the young to the Spanish landscape or to the origins of analytical thought.

The citizens of Munich could not ignore Ortega, although the city fathers, ignoring a campaign in the Munich press, did not make him an honorary citizen. The Bavarian Academy of Fine Arts seized the opportunity to make him a member. Marburg, the town of Ortega's first German residence, did itself honor by giving him an honorary law degree, as did the University of Glasgow. All these events took place in 1951, the year in which Ortega was obliged to interrupt his journey from London to Munich and spend a week in Paris, waiting for the arrival of his luggage, which had been misrouted. Could it have been an irony of fate, punishing him for having passed through France too rapidly in former years? But Ortega, as always on occasions of enforced leisure, quietly withdrew into his hotel room, worked on his manuscripts, brewed his coffee, and enjoyed the second stimulus, the ever-present cigarette.

Gradually, Germany became accustomed to his comings and goings. When Ortega once more boarded the plane for Madrid, on 7 March 1952, he was allowed to leave without any public notice, an inconspicuous intellectual of considerable caliber. Before his departure he told the Germans: "No people ever perished of its catastrophes. At most, it perished of calcification. We are in the midst of a transition toward entirely new conditions and situations. The Germans will live through it." Yet one thing gave him pause: "When you look at them—if only they had never to deal with political matters!—when you look at them and see with what energy and tenacity they labor, you sometimes get the feeling that these are not men at work, but ants!" Once more, Ortega proved himself excellent as *el espectador*.

On the occasion of Karl Jaspers's seventieth birthday, a festchrift was published in Munich. Although Ortega never met Jaspers, his coeval and no doubt the single German thinker whose mind was most akin to Ortega's own, he contributed an essay in which he discussed the pre-Socratics, whose thought, close to that of both men, should be rediscovered by our age.

In that same year, 1953, Ortega took part in another of the Darmstadt Colloquia, dealing this time with the subject of "Man and Organization." In the press coverage of the event, Ortega was granted first place among the many participants from six foreign countries, and his brilliant aphorisms were widely quoted. The event was a feeble rearguard action of intellectuals in rebellion against technology and statism, "progress" and massification, and Ortega stood out as still the most vigorous and experienced guerilla fighter. In this battle, he won the palm of victory. E. Schulz wrote: "Not one of the participants could offer a prescription without a moralistic or religious admixture. Ortega alone, who fought the battle on his own strength, with cold-blooded irony, was the exception to this." Back in Spain, Ortega's countrymen shared in the triumphs in distant Germany of "our greatest thinker" (*Información Española,* 24 October 1953).

On other occasions, Ortega showed himself capable of impish mischief, and of confounding sponsors and audiences alike, as he did at the Centro Italiano in Munich, in a debate on "Apocalypse and History." Ortega, a panel member of the conference, spoke twice as long as the main speaker, the historian Franz Altheim, using up all the time intended for discussion.

One performance especially surprising and disappointing to his many admirers in Germany was his delivery of a philosophical paper on dance and masquerades during a visit to the carnival in Munich in February 1954. He attended it with his good friend and namesake, the bullfighter Domingo Ortega. Even his international reputation did not protect him from ridicule.

Another event that occasioned disappointment to his admirers came from his speech on the "sportive-festive meaning of life," delivered in February 1954, at the plenary session of the German Athletic Association in Düsseldorf. "Those who were looking to this brilliant mind for light on the present situation in the world of sports were sadly disappointed," the reporters wrote. Was it out of season, or was it the wrong place, to recall the lasting contribution of Johan Huizinga's *homo ludens*? Ortega, never athletically inclined himself, felt an inner kinship with athletes because he himself was an athlete of the mind par excellence and, as a practicing philosopher, "the best example of pointless activity." But was there anyone in the German republic, the country of the economic miracle, characterized by its fanatic striving for improvement, who could take seriously Ortega's thesis that "work is a derivative, an offspring of sports"? Only a Latin could cast doubt on the proposition that "life needs a challenge," and maintain that "life is essentially a sporting contest."

On the other hand, the Germans were pleased to hear Ortega's other remark: that the German people were the only young people in all Europe, a people who had the greatest epoch in their history still before them. "The Germans have the greatest driving power; but they lack brakes." Germany's women, Ortega said, could act as such brakes: they were the great appeasers. The words ring with the sounds of German classicism and romanticism; and they presented an odd challenge to the German administrators and managers, among whom Ortega the realist-idealist could secure no more than a small *succès d'estime*. His complimentary remarks about the Germans could not make them forget their disappointment that Ortega had shirked his responsibility as historian. "Who would have expected this of him?" the press complained. Yet anyone who knew Ortega's writings, all of which had sidestepped historiology for over a decade, anyone who had heard his Madrid lectures since 1945, or had read his essays, would have expected just this.

In his varied and active life, Ortega suffered many disappointments and defeats. Even these last six noisy and fame-filled years in Germany were no exception. He obtained much public notice, including a reception by his fellow author, president of the Federal Republic, Theodor Heuss. But there was little action to implement the reforms Ortega advocated. Nothing came of the secretly longed-for guest professorship at the University of Munich, nor of his project to establish in Hamburg a German branch of his Institute for the Humanities, nor of his plans for the reform of university teaching that was so desperately needed. In a polemic written earlier and published in Munich in 1952 under the title "Guilt and Responsibility of the University," Ortega rejected the narrow specialization prevalent among university professors, and instead called for broad generalists on the university lecterns. At the center of the *universitas litterarum* he proposed, there was to be a "theory of culture" limited in subject matter and divided into five disciplines.

Though many were impressed by this new Erasmus, others (such as B. Freudenfeld) raised the question "on what anthropology, that is, on what theology, is this program based?" Europe as the guiding intelligence, the humanistic sciences as the cure—"that is just half a diagnosis, half a therapy. The sole rule of these sciences was, is, and always will be a sham rule." The valiant advocate of this sham seemed like a belated spokesman of the Enlightenment, his doctrine like the

best but no longer convincing extension of the eighteenth and nineteenth centuries into the changing
twentieth.

But it would be simplistic and indeed unfair to
leave this final impression of Ortega as high-spirited
and yet a failure, a *torero* of the mind in Germany's
intellectual arena, a man with nothing more to his
credit than his bravado and fine escapades. Ortega was
the acknowledged darling of the public lecture hall no
less than of the private gathering, one of those distinguished comforters and admonishers from abroad
who came to Germany after 1945 in order to reprove,
inform, and reassure the humiliated nation. We may
recall such "lions of the meeting hall and star performers of scholarly conventions" as André Gide or
Edouard Mounier, T. S. Eliot, Victor Gollancz, Thorn-
ton Wilder, or Arnold Toynbee, who came to Germany like mighty wizards from distant lands after the
spiritual isolation of Hitler's Thousand-year Reich
had come to an end, to harvest the breathless attention
of large audiences. Ortega, a kindred spirit brought up
on German philosophy, was one of these great comforters who came to inspire the deeply confused and
helpless Germans with new courage. His brilliant public style has been described to perfection by a compe-
tent observer, the Protestant Bishop Hans Lilje. In his
*Sonntagsblatt,* published in Hamburg, Lilje wrote:

When he enters the lecture hall, he exudes that unmistakable and indescribable aura surrounding a great man.
Everyone in the audience knows that a thinker of world
renown has entered, and Ortega himself knows it. But, and
this is highly characteristic of him, he knows it in his own
sovereign way. Like all the others, he is totally aware and
conscious of it, but there is no need to talk about it. There
is then not a trace of any of those poses men strike to under-

line their importance. The self-assurance with which he accepts the fame he has earned makes all such attitudes unnecessary. Nothing artificial, forced, or unnatural. Fame fits this aged gentleman like a well-tailored suit. The only unexpected feature in his appearance is that he is of short stature, like Napoleon. All else is just about as one would have expected: an imposing cranium, the high forehead of the intellectual, all other facial features—mouth, nose, ears —of generous proportions. Skin like parchment. And, above all, a compelling voice, not loud but sonorous. His German with its foreign accent is a delight to hear. After a few even-tempered sentences, his speech breaks forth, again and again, in this or that spirited sally, his eyes flash with intellectual excitement, and rare indeed is the lecture in which he does not treat us to flashes of beautiful and vigorous humor.

Let this, then, be the image lingering in our memories of Germany's great friend and adviser.

Ortega's visits to Germany, his lecture tours, eagerly undertaken and gladly extended, are to be understood as a part of his "journey into the past," a return to his old loves: his own youth in Germany, and Germany's new youth at work among the ruins. No permanent professional or personal ties came out of these visits. But were they not also perhaps a flight from Spain, an escape to Europe? In Spain, Ortega could hope for and accomplish even less than in the economically stronger and more active, and intellectually fermenting, West Germany.

Ortega's Institute for the Humanities in Madrid— or, as we may reformulate the name, his Academy for a Theory of Culture on Historical Foundations—did not, and could not, flourish. His worldwide fame did not enable him to penetrate to the hearts of his postwar countrymen. Ortega the ten-year absentee was so far in thinking and historical experience from those

Spaniards who had stayed on in Spain throughout the great upheaval that most Spaniards, especially the younger people, grew ever more apart from him and tended to look on him with mounting amazement and distrust.

Spain, however, gladly shared in Ortega's public triumphs in Germany and in the new world. Spain was delighted when English men of letters, among whom was Alan Pryce-Jones, editor of the *Times Literary Supplement,* urged that Ortega be awarded the Nobel Prize and were backed in their suggestion by the South American and the Swedish press. But "Spain's turn" did not come until 1956, after Ortega's death, when the prize was awarded to the poet of genius, Juan Ramón Jiménez. In 1950, Jiménez, though himself being touted for the Nobel Prize, had generously and ardently supported Ortega's candidacy. It was unjust toward Spain to pass over its outstanding intellects, Unamuno, Baroja y Nessi, Ortega, in favor of the Icelander Halldór Laxness or the English statesman Winston Churchill. This was done despite the fact that men around the world who knew Spain well, even British Jesuits, championed Ortega in the press and on the radio as "one of the most original and important thinkers of our time."

From Germany's lecture halls Ortega occasionally returned to his study in Madrid, and to his family, his friends, and his steadily growing and by now internationally famous publishing house. From his strenuous efforts in public to reform life he would come home to the privacy of silent self-examination and quiet self-expression. Over his desk in Madrid hung a large picture of Chateaubriand, whom Ortega revered, along with Goethe, as the great exemplar of literary style, and Goethe's works stood within easy reach.

On 18 October 1955, this rich and full and extraordinary life came to an end. That same year death had reaped a bitter toll among the world's great minds: Paul Claudel, Henri Matisse, Pierre Teilhard de Chardin, Albert Einstein, and Thomas Mann had gone to their rest.

During the summer, Ortega, as was his custom, went to the north of Spain. He was unaware that a mortal cancer was destroying him from within. In the early fall he confidently placed himself under doctors' care, but the physicians soon found their resources of little avail.

For almost three weeks, into mid-October, bulletins about Ortega's health appeared in every Spanish newspaper as news of national importance. Even the foreign press showed concern for his fate. His ideological critics held their peace. Ortega himself, cheerful and confident, chatted with his many visitors, in which he indulged in his etymological hobby, smoked —and rapidly became weaker. Father Félix García, an Augustinian and friend of the Ortega family, was often alone with Ortega during those weeks, and what they talked about remains their secret.

Before death Ortega was granted absolution by Father García, though it is not known if he was con-

scious when he received it. Father García also assumed
the responsibility of sponsoring a Catholic funeral,
with burial in consecrated ground, the churchyard of
San Isidro in Madrid, for Ortega. Usually, recanting of
his antireligious writings would be the prerequisite
demanded for these privileges, but it is not known
whether Ortega did indeed disclaim his lifetime position. On the basis of reports of his private conversations, however, one can safely affirm that Ortega occu-
pied himself increasingly with religious matters in his
last years.

Many native and foreign commentators interpreted the funeral as the ultimate capitulation of a
fearsome freethinker and praised him accordingly.
Ortega's own sons remained absent from the official
mass for the dead.

This episode affords a particularly revealing insight into the Spanish enigma, especially if we keep in
mind that at that time Joaquín Ruiz Jiménez—a practicing Catholic, Spain's minister of education, former
ambassador to the Vatican, and son of a liberal monarchist—was a regular visitor to Ortega's home, and
that even the Archbishop of Saragossa came to visit
the sick Ortega, only to find him dying.

On the other hand, a secret, almost triumphant
whisper ran through Madrid, where diehard nonconformists of various persuasions and shades, in the cof-
feehouses and bookstores, salons and *tertulias,* pos-
tured as if they had won a victory. They claimed what
they had no right to claim and indeed no way of
knowing: "He did not give in!" Ortega's last days hold
a mystery. What gives it special significance is that it
illustrates Spain's internal dilemma.

All of the obituaries written in honor of the dead
Ortega, eloquent as they were, cannot make us forget

the truth of the words Ortega himself had written, in an anonymous article published in the newspaper *El Sol* in 1920, after the death of the great liberal writer and historian Benito Pérez Galdós: "Official Spain, cold, dry, and protocol-ridden, remained aloof from that unanimous expression of sorrow caused by Galdós's death. The visit of the minister of education was not enough."

But the response of unofficial Spain to Ortega's death was all the more impressive and diverse. There were, of course, the dutiful expressions of appreciation, but low-keyed tones of reserve and even outright antagonism were perceptible from the very beginning.

On 19 October 1955, the day after Ortega's death, the Falangist Party organ *Arriba* devoted five pages to Ortega's memory. Ortega's friends among philosophers, men of letters, and men of science offered their homilies on these pages. But even then Adolfo Muñóz Alonso, Christian philosopher and director of the journals *Crisis* and *Augustinas,* challenged Marías's right to call Ortega "Spain's greatest philosopher," deploring the fact that the classical themes of philosophy —soul, world, transcendence, God—had not been covered in Ortega's philosophy because ratiovitalism had other goals and methods. Ponce de León publicly regretted the absence of religion in Ortega's work. But far more eloquent than mere words was the republication of a photograph of Ortega delivering his first public lecture after his return from exile, in Madrid's Ateneo in 1946, "when others had forsaken us" (that is, when Spain was being excluded by the United Nations according to the ruling that only nations that had declared war on Germany before the fall of Berlin could become members).

Also on 19 October 1955, *ABC,* Spain's leading

newspaper, monarchist, Catholic, and liberal in orientation, published eleven pages in homage including statements by Spain's best minds. Particularly noteworthy were the articles by Ortega's former student Xavier Zubiri, a lay theologian and ex-scholastic, who was to round out Ortega's philosophical thinking and then enlarge it; by his favorite among his students, the polemical Julián Marías; and by Ortega's physicians and his housekeeper. Only the still fresh impact of the loss can explain the claim of Gregorio Marañón, a fine dermatologist, political liberal, and splendid essayist, that in Ortega the world had lost "its greatest intellect." Father Félix García poured oil on the waters, then hardly perceptible, of the orthodox Catholic opposition with this fundamental statement: "From an intelligence as extraordinary and from a heart as deep as Ortega's, God cannot have been far. Let us not try to pierce the mystery of God, and of the infinite forgivingness of death. . . ."

The Orthodox Catholic daily *YA* found itself in the most difficult position of all. On the day of Ortega's death, 18 October, *YA* had published a high-minded, self-critical poem by a young priest and poet, Martín Descalzo, entitled "Prayer for Don José." The poem does not absolve Spanish Catholicism of its failure to keep Ortega in its fold. Not enough prayers had been offered asking that Ortega overcome his pride; the example of Christianity set before him had been "rickety," lacking the graces that could have attracted his beauty-intoxicated eyes. On 19 October Joaquín Ruiz Jiménez, then minister of education, published his memorial: "May he rest in peace!" He urged a "respectful truce," but did not attempt to play down the radical differences between the people of prewar Spain and postwar Spain. On 20 October,

*YA* offered its readers a listing and appraisal of Ortega's writings.

In the 19 October 1955 *ABC* issue, the Catholic journalist Bartolomé Mostaza stressed Ortega's "absolute secularism," but he excused his religious insensitivity on the grounds that he had lacked information and examples, and that his upbringing had been unfavorable. Stressing the fact that Ortega had been influenced in his youth by the freethinkers Ernst Renan and Alfred Loisy, he titled his essay: "A Child of His Time Rather than His Free Will."

But many of the seemingly neutral articles had unmistakably edged undertones. Among these were such articles as that published in Ortega's home town that used the weapon of damning with faint praise; it described him as *"el gran prosista"* (the great prose stylist). Elsewhere he was labeled as the author of *Invertebrate Spain,* the controversial volume of essays in which he had treated Spain most mercilessly. Ignorance or intent?

The first obituaries were followed by tributes to and analyses of Ortega's works in all the important and unimportant journals of the nation—from the leading literary reviews *Insula* and *Indice* to the student publication *Alcalá,* which closed its eightieth and final issue with a memorial to Ortega. Their healthy, young skepticism kept the students from spouting blind adulation, though they lamented, "Alas Ortega that the time has come to eulogize you."

Some of the young Falangists took a pretty dim view of Ortega. They saw him as the intellectual antagonist of the "factually more correct" Marcelino Menéndez y Pelayo, who had been the standard bearer of conservative traditionalism, and reduced Ortega even then to the status of a "secondary mind" who

had been right only in minor matters. Ortega had
been a disappointment, it was claimed, when he returned to Spain, because his mind had stopped in the
year 1930, and he had failed to rid himself of his old
clique of disciples. The dialogue that he resumed in
1945 was with this clique, not with the youth of Spain.

Could Ortega's admirers console themselves with
the splendidly presented special edition of the literary
journal *Insula,* devoted to a commemoration of Ortega by Marías and one of his South American disciples? Or with the luxuriously illustrated special issue
of *Indice,* which captured Ortega's life in superb pho-
tographs?

Meanwhile, a flood of condolences kept arriving
from abroad and were gladly accepted as proof of
Spain's prestige beyond its borders. The message from
the German Federal Republic struck the most personal note. It was delivered by West Germany's first
ambassador to Spain, Prince Adalbert of Bavaria, son
of a Spanish infanta, who stood in the front rank of
official mourners at Ortega's funeral. Ortega's death
meant an irreparable loss to Germany as well! The
same sentiment inspired the telegrams of West Germany's president, Theodor Heuss, alluding to the
"friendly and grateful memory" of his meeting with
Ortega, and of the German chancellor, Konrad Ade-
nauer. The newspaper *ABC* reported memorial ser-
vices for Ortega in Hamburg and in Frankfurt and reminded readers that only two years earlier he had
been invited to return to Germany.

In England, the cognoscenti recalled that the utopian socialist H. G. Wells had been one of the many
enthusiastic champions of *The Revolt of the Masses,*
and that the historian Arnold J. Toynbee had been
Ortega's frequent companion. Obituaries in the

United States prompted Spain's ambassador in Washington to protest energetically to the *New York Times* that Spain had been a European nation even without Ortega and before him. Argentina rejoiced that Ortega had so often sought its hospitality and had thought of himself as "half-Argentinian."

The Italian response came last. It found its way to Madrid two weeks after Ortega's death. Half a dozen of Italy's leading writers paid tribute to Ortega, but unanimously concluded that his life showed hardly any contacts with Spain's neighbor and former rival Italy. The ingrained realism of the Mediterranean, furthermore, led the Italians to arrive at a fresh insight not reached in other European countries. Ortega, the Italians pointed out, had been a fundamentally political man, and as such, more doomed to meet disappointments throughout his life than humanists, writers, and thinkers are. Spanish commentators regarded this unanimity of the Italians as a monotonous cliché; to me, it seems an indication of the acumen of culturally akin, qualified observers.

Within Spain in the weeks after Ortega's death, criticism was muted by that academic courtesy and style to which a departed professor of Spain's greatest university was entitled. This academic courtesy found its most attractive expression exactly one month after Ortega's death in the memorial service of the impressive Central University of Madrid. While not the oldest, it is certainly the most prestigious of Spain's institutions of higher learning. In the somber, formal hall of the philosophical faculty, one cool and sunless November morning, thousands of students and hundreds of faculty members gathered to pay moving tribute to their dead colleague and teacher. The seven speakers were all colleagues or former students of Ortega, and most of them were on the university faculty. Three or four of the speakers are particularly deserving of notice. One of these was the student speaker, who, though reaffirming that his generation had had no contact with Ortega, expressed his admiration for the man, as a mysterious phenomenon, now gone, who had challenged the young to "solitary experience and personal adventure." The audience waited in great suspense to see how the next speaker, González Alvarez, a neoscholastic appointed to succeed Ortega despite his radically different views, would maintain the delicate balance between respect and candor: González Alvarez succeeded so well that the most critical member of the audience, Ortega's old friend and comrade-at-arms Marañón, was moved to express his full and sincere agreement with González Alvarez's comments. Marañón himself gave a memorial address that turned out to be a personal declaration of his liberal convictions.

A passage in Marañón's address deserves special notice, because it claimed Ortega as a Spaniard. It is not easy to define a native of Castile, one raised in the South of Spain, grown to human and intellectual maturity in Germany, and shaped by fate into a citizen of Europe and the world. Where lie the roots of such a man? Where is his native soil? Ortega himself had always acknowledged his Spanish heritage, but had with equal fervor asserted the German elements in his intellectual makeup. In consequence, he had occasionally been chided for being "half German," a reproach that found its most bitter expression in the then current invective *"primer filósofo de España, quinto de Alemania"* (Spain's first philosopher, and Germany's fifth).

About this Marañón said:

Ortega's national passion had its roots in those deeper strata that lie beneath the surface of modern Spain. Throughout his work we encounter passages revealing his understanding and sympathy for those old, extinct tribes. Even his humanity shows such traces. Like other intellectual leaders, Ortega cannot be assigned to this or that particular Spanish landscape. Only when we sound the innermost depths of this man do we encounter those layers that are combined, stratum upon stratum, in his human existence.

Most convincing, perhaps, is the view that sees him as an Andalusian, from that region of upper Andalusia where the Guadalquivir river still carries Castilian sand down to Cordoba, the Andalusia that gave birth to the philosophers and poets of the Caliphate.* Ortega makes us think also of that other Andalusia, the region of Málaga with its face set toward Africa, its mysterious antiquity, the region that saw the sun rise over those arid lands that Rome had broken to the plow, where the impetuous spirit of Saint Augustine burst into flame and left fiery traces that would still illumine the eloquence and intellectual fire of men such as Ortega y Gasset.

González Alvarez warned against the danger of an "Ortega scholasticism," a reduction and misconstruction of Ortega's highly personal statement into grist for the academic mill. As a thinker, Alvarez said, Ortega reaches into our day.

There is perhaps a touch of self-glorification in the closing words of Pedro Laín Entralgo, dean of the university, medical historian of many accomplishments, who was considered a staunch follower of Or-

*The Roman Seneca and the Jew Maimonides were natives of Cordoba, as was the Arab Averröes, whose world view bears certain similarities to that of Ortega. Karl Vossler, Germany's great romance scholar, had spoken of Ortega as a "second Averröes."

tega. He claimed that an ideal, universal Spain had now emerged, in virtue of the harmony between the philosophy of Thomas Aquinas and that of Ortega! Must these words not have sounded like outright heresy to many Spanish Catholics? In any case, the indignation in Madrid at Laín Entralgo's bold remark did not die down for many weeks.

Ten days after the celebration at the university, dignified and conciliatory though in certain details perhaps somewhat acerbic, there followed incidents of a less balanced nature. They gave rise to such rumors as that, on 29 November, at the Instituto Internacional in Madrid, the police had forbidden the playing of recordings of Ortega's speeches. Marías, Ortega's indefatigable champion, delivered his panegyric on Ortega to a select group, describing him as the embodiment "of the most important intellectual and philosophical new direction of the century." Such exaggerations inevitably provoked sobering rejoinders. The truce concluded over Ortega's bier was now ready to collapse.

In December 1955 Miranda Vicente, suffragan of Toledo, gave a speech, "What We Have Not Been Told about Ortega," in which he dealt with Ortega's role under the second Spanish republic, with his qualifications as an educator for our day, and with the distinction that had to be made between the man and his work. Miranda Vicente's speech had been preceded by similar statements from the spiritual council of the Frente de Juventudes (national youth association). Three months later, a pastoral letter from the top Spanish clergy struck the same note, by stating that atheists and materialists, skeptics and relativists, were unfit to be teachers of the youth of Spain. The devout universalist Marcelino Menéndez y Pelayo,

himself a "one-man academy," was held up as the
model teacher. Piety toward Ortega faded into the
background, and Spain's fiery intellectual battle,
the battle between progress and tradition that had been
raging for more than a century, resumed in all its
fury. It is a conflict of such depth that even death cannot repress it for more than a few passing moments.

Looking back over the 1950s we see that the controversy over Ortega's philosophical position and the
value of his work had in fact been gathering for several years before his death. Let us recall here that,
from 1938 to 1951, it is generally agreed that Franco's
cultural policies were strictly conservative, entirely in
harmony with the political views of the Catholic
church. Then, from 1951 onward, a more compromis-
ing attitude began to emerge—one that exhibited a
measure of respect for those opponents of the regime
who held to different basic principles, or who had held
to such principles during their lives, and for their
followers. Among these we may count intransigent
traditionalists such as Unamuno and Ortega, liberals
such as Madariaga and Menéndez Pidal, as well as the
revolutionary poets García Lorca and Miguel Hernández. The appointments of Laín Entralgo and Tovar, both followers of Ortega, to deanships at the
universities of Madrid and Salamanca, were a clear expression of this direction. To the slowly retreating
right wing, the impressive series of lectures offered in
Madrid in 1953 in honor of Ortega's seventieth birthday, on the very practical subject "The Present Situation" ("El estado de la cuestión") represented the crowning event in the cultural offensive of the faction of
compromise.

The counterattack came in the spring of 1953.

It opened the battle over Ortega's contribution to thought. In its May 1953 issue (Number 89), official Spain's most important cultural periodical, *Arbor,* edited by Vicente Marrero, a long-standing, bitter opponent of Ortega's, published several contributions that added fuel to the spreading fire. That issue reflects an important event in Spain's cultural life, and therefore deserves to be looked at. A thorough study of this issue is absolutely necessary to an understanding of Ortega's role in Spain's cultural life since the civil war. All the alignments, all the emerging viewpoints of the future, are discernible in this issue.

The substance of the matter is as follows:

Professor Cruz Hernández of Salamanca, who wrote "The Future of Spanish Philosophy," expressed his confidence that there was such a future, thanks to the ceaseless educational labors of Manuel García Morente, Ortega's neo-Kantian companion and colleague at the Central University of Madrid. Long an atheist, he had reconverted to Catholicism while an expatriate in France. He later returned to Spain and had become a priest before he died in 1942. And Cruz Hernández also praised the intellectual achievements of Xavier Zubiri, "Spain's best philosophic mind . . . since Suarez." (Marías, incidentally, had made the same claim for Ortega.)

Then followed a favorable review by Pujals of a biography by García Morente.

The real call to battle of the issue, however, is in a few lines of commentary by Vicente Marrero, saying the lecture series arranged by Ortega's friends should be disqualified because they were an ineffectual attempt to honor the work of a man who, despite his many accomplishments, had conjured up within the last five decades "the most intelligent, most system-

atic, and most brilliant attempt to dechristianize
Spain."

Before the month was up, ten well-known followers of Ortega raised their voices in protest against this
"total, massive falsification that cannot be tolerated."

In August 1953, Marrero declared his own position
in the matter by placing Ortega in the same category
of thinkers as Rudolf Bultmann, Protestant theologian
of the University of Marburg and famed as the "de-
mythologizer of Christianity," and Friedrich Nietzsche.
In support of his accusation of Ortega's relationship
to the church, Marrero cited two university deans and
the Archbishop of Granada.

Abated only momentarily by Ortega's death, the
battle rages to this day.

The years 1958 and 1959 saw a high point in the
Ortega controversy. I shall quote some of the more
striking utterances because, due to the absence of
lively political controversies, this battle has long been
one of the most revealing indexes of Spanish intellectual life. I shall pass over in silence a good number of
provincial and pedantic criticasters or meddling dilettantes. They are only fringe happenings around the
central issue, which is this: one of the leading, and
perhaps *the* leading cultural power in Spain, the Catholic church, through spokesmen who raised their
voices spontaneously rather than in obedience to in-
structions from "on high," voiced publicly the church's
reservations against Ortega and his influence.

According to Marías, the anti-Ortega campaign
began with the "Jesuit conspiracy" of 1942, when a
Jesuit of Madrid, Joaquín Iriarte, published the first
Ortega biography: a critical and basically unsympa-
thetic though not wholly unappreciative collection of
excerpts from Ortega's writings, annotated almost too

conscientiously with passages from Spanish and foreign commentaries. It lacked any genuine comparative
research into the sources of Ortega's original work.

It was followed in 1943 by the more penetrating,
though much shorter, study by Sánchez Villaseñor, a
Jesuit from Mexico, who wrote his work in Mexico
in 1943 as a doctoral dissertation, and published it in
1949 in English, in Chicago. Villaseñor's work is mark-
edly philosophical in tenor, clearly antagonistic, and
without the least understanding of the evolution of
Ortega's thought in the course of his life.

It would, however, be easy to refute Marías's no-
tion of a "conspiracy" by citing German and English
sources because Jesuits in those countries struck a
much milder, much more tolerant tone when dealing
with Ortega. The Spaniard will invariably reply that
the "Spanish problem" does not have the same ur-
gency north of the Pyrenees, and that the Spanish
people must suffer the full brunt of it and break their
hearts, while others merely sympathize.

In 1953, a tolerant but altogether ironical and
critical antagonism was expressed in *Six Glosses on
Ortega's Philosophy*, a tome of three hundred fifty-
eight pages by the Franciscan Miguel Oromí. Oromí
did not base his thinking on Catholic dogma; Aris-
totelian logic was his sole weapon in this attack
aimed at Ortega's leading disciple, Marías, and his
ratiovitalistic followers, rather than at Ortega himself.

After this satirical interlude in the Catholic offensive came another thunderbolt, hurled from the
ranks of the Dominicans. In 1958 appeared what was
up to that time the most important and most exhaus-
tive work on Ortega's philosophy, by Santiago Ramírez, who worked at Rome and Freiburg and was, at the
time he wrote his book, professor at the University of

Salamanca. Resting its case firmly on scholasticism and orthodox dogma, the book offers the first critical synthesis of Ortega's entire oeuvre, but it fails to appreciate and evaluate the several phases in the intellectual growth and development of Ortega's thought. Besides, the aged Ramírez's long absence from his native Spain seems to have left its mark upon his analysis.

In answer to these massive attacks, one after the other of Ortega's friends rose to the defense with a number of shorter essays. Articles and brochures attacking the aims and methodology of the militant Father Ramírez came from the pens of the following: Laín Entralgo, former dean of Madrid; José Aranguren, professor of ethics at Madrid, with *Ortega's Ethics* (1958, 62 pages); the historian José Antonio Maravall, with *Ortega and the Present Situation* (1959, 53 pages); and Marías, who by now had drifted away from academic life.

Before the end of 1958, Father Ramírez countered with a rejoinder full of wit and fighting spirit. In 1959 he refuted Marías's shorter essay *The Danger Point* (1958, 43 pages) in his much larger *Safety Zone* (309 pages), in which he called Marías "the last of Ortega's epigones," and once more compared Ortega unfavorably with Thomas Aquinas. But even the journal *Religión y Cultura,* published by the Augustinian Order at their university, the Escorial, printed an anonymous essay in opposition to Father Ramírez. Ortega's work, it can be seen, aroused conflicting responses within Spain's heart of hearts, the church. It would be unrealistic to hope that *l'affaire* Ortega will ever be settled by convoking a national meeting of Spain's philosophers.

The type and timing of blow and counterblow were frequently determined by political events. The policy of cultural liberalization, beginning in the early 1950s and passionately opposed by militant traditionalists since 1953, had started out with revisionist publications and corresponding appointments to cultural key positions. Widespread unrest among university students followed; violent disturbances continued at the Central University of Madrid. Franco, apparently with good reason, feared strong infiltration of leftist elements into the academic professions, and put on the brakes: influential deans, government appointees, and the minister of education were replaced in 1955 and 1956, and the monarchists and traditionalists in the cabinet were given broader powers.

A close observer might have noticed a curious parallelism of events in the spring of 1956, which threw the sharp ideological conflicts within the academic world into sudden relief:

On 20 May 1956, Gregorio Marañón, a dilettante in many spheres of intellectual endeavor and well-known militant liberal, was received into the Academy of the Fine Arts; it was the fifth time in his life that the academic community had conferred distinctions upon him. The ceremony took place in the ancient, dim, and cramped San Fernando auditorium in Madrid. His acceptance speech, delivered approximately to five hundred guests, only two hundred of whom could be seated in the packed hall, dealt with a chapter of his studies of the painter El Greco. He rejected the spirit of Philip II and the intolerance of the Escorial, and instead gave praise to the Christian-Islamic-Judaic symbiosis of Toledo. He offered an encomium for El Greco of Toledo, Italianized Greek who became a true Spaniard, the prototype of the enlightened "new Christian." This address could be interpreted as Marañón's rejection, the third within the year, of the official cultural ideology of the state, and as a further gesture of friendship for Ortega.

On the very next day, at the Ateneo, Rafael Calvo Serer, the ousted moving spirit of the journal *Arbor,* was heard for the first time after almost three years of enforced silence, with a referendum on "the present dialectic of the Spanish image." Close to a hundred persons, among whom were a rowdy group of Falangist opponents, came to hear his second attack on religious and cultural "heterodoxy," his advocacy of European conservatism, and his open declaration of opposition to Ortega, whom he mentioned by name.

The same ideas that Marañón had presented under the guise of art-history reflections were offered in plain language by Dionisio Ridruejo, former Falangist, poet, an inner emigrant. Ortega, Ridruejo stated, was sound. His thinking was much needed now as a "balanced mind, a friend of order, an enemy of demagoguery." The polemics surrounding Ortega clearly concerned not just ideological disagreements but the future governing of Spain.

Philosophers are attempting to identify the true, authentic Ortega; others are searching for Ortega the patriot, who first and foremost and almost without exception used his pen in behalf of his country. There is always more at stake in the Ortega controversy than mere journalistic skirmishes or so-called monastic feuds. We would be seriously misled if we tried to judge the matter by looking only, for example, at the 1958 volume of the monthly *Punta Europa,* a publication as important as *Arbor* though rather more *au courant.* This volume appeared under the editorship of Vicente Marrero, the man who first opened the Ortega controversy in 1953. A former student of Heidegger at Freiburg, Marrero devoted four issues of his periodical to a massive attack on Ortega. He even called on José Gaos of Mexico, Ortega's collaborator in the days before Marías, for intellectual support; and he adroitly profited from the occasion to establish the reputation of his Spanish ally Father Ramírez, who, owing to his long residence abroad, was not sufficiently well known and appreciated in Spain. These preliminary articles were later developed into Marrero's militant volume of essays *Ortega, Philosopher of Fashion* (1961, 355 pages), in which the theatrical posing, the pathos, and the modernity of Ortega "the thinker" were exposed, documented, and commented upon; a volume, in short, which undertook to demythologize the Spanish "Ortega myth."

But let us not neglect what followed. Until 1956, Ruiz Jiménez, a former student of Ortega and sympathetic to him, held the post of minister of education in Madrid's cabinet. By February of 1957, however, that cabinet included a known opponent of Ortega, partisan of the conservative monarchist faction: he was General Jorge Vigón, minister for public works. Vigón did not devote his life wholly to military service. He was also a writer and frequent public speaker. In 1957, he had seized the opportunity of Menéndez y Pelayo's centenary to expound his views, views wholly in harmony with those of the Spanish church hierarchy, and to make a critical comparison of Menéndez y Pelayo's traditional ideals with those of Ortega the liberal reformer.

The power of Ortega's mind and spirit thus made itself felt even after his death in the highest spheres of Spanish political life. His influence left its mark also on seminal works of Spanish scholarship. One example of this is the literary studies of the world-renowned philologist and scholar, Dámaso Alonso. An even more striking example is the history of political ideas of Luis Diez del Corral and the reflections on art of Lafuente Ferrari. But most important are the two watershed works of twentieth-century Spanish historiography. I do not speak of the research into medieval epic and romance done by the venerable president of the academy, Ramón Menéndez Pidal, doyen of Spanish historians, but of two towering works of Spanish expatriates of the generation after Pidal. From Mexico came Américo Castro's *Spain and Its History: Christians, Moors, and Jews* (first published in 1948; revised edition, 1954, *The True History of Spain*). This book is among the most powerful documents of "the other Spain," the Spain in exile. Much in the spirit of Ortega, Castro denied that the Visigoths had any genuine influence upon Spanish culture, and ascribed all of Spain's cultural achievements to the Arabs and the Jews. Castro, who was a professor at an American university when he wrote the work, openly admitted that he was speaking not just as an historian but equally as a political partisan and philosopher. His opponents quickly took up the challenge—too quickly, perhaps, for adequate scholarly preparation. In 1956, the leading Spanish medievalist, the expatriate Claudio Sánchez Albornoz, published his two-volume work *Spain, Historical Enigma* (1487 pages), in which he treated Castro's, and thus Ortega's, convictions with respect, but utterly refuted the historical documentation on which they rest.

For better or worse, then: Spain must govern herself with or against Ortega, she must pursue the sciences and the arts with or against him. Ortega's ghost walks across Spain in broad daylight, and his spirit, even more than his language, is alive today. And it will remain alive for a long time yet.

More than fifteen years have gone by since Ortega died, ten years since this study first appeared in its original German version. The passage of time has only served to increase Ortega's stature.

The controversies surrounding Ortega have by now lost much of their earlier bitterness. Franco's Spain, kingdom without a king, has entered upon a phase of economic growth and political liberalization, in which ideological conflicts tend to soften. Father Santiago Ramírez, formerly the leader of the attacks on Ortega on account of his religious and metaphysical unorthodoxy, has remained silent, but his militancy has been revived by Vicente Marrero. Marrero's long volume *The Spanish Civil War and the Brain Trust* (1961, 683 pages) did not, however, have an impact despite Marrero's considerable scholarship, owing to its diffuseness and vehement intolerance. The work may be regarded as the final sally in an ideological offensive that ranked Menéndez y Pelayo, José Antonio Primo de Rivera, and Ramiro de Maeztu as the standardbearers of Spain's spiritual renewal, and called Ortega a "dangerous physician at Spain's sickbed," concerned primarily with "preserving Spain's decadence." But the book's appearance could not rekindle the old battle. Ortega's disciples and supporters simply ignored it.

Another book, also published in 1961, proved more effective. This was Gonzalo Fernández de la Mora's collection of essays, *Ortega and the Generation of '98*, a fiery work by Marrero's antagonist of long standing. It was so well received that it went into a second printing before the year's end. Fernández de la Mora belongs to a younger generation of intellectuals than those defenders of Ortega whom we have discussed earlier—Marías, Laín Entralgo, Aranguren, and the others. Once an admirer of Ortega, Fernández de la Mora had become disenchanted with his former hero after the civil war. But something of Ortega's rationality and stylistic brilliance had rubbed off on him. After years of intensive study of Ortega's writings he came to the conclusion that Ortega had been "the greatest thinker in Hispanic culture during the first half of the twentieth century, and one of the world's most important thinkers of the era." Yet even in Fernández de la Mora's view, Ortega belongs to the past. He sees him primarily as an authoritarian, conservative-liberal patriot in the tradition of enlightened despotism, a man of contradictions and powerful intuitions, given to metaphorical rather than systematic thinking. The book is excellently documented and splendidly written. It is beyond a doubt one of the best works on Ortega to come from Spain's right-wing intelligentsia.

Mention must be made also of a book published in Mexico, in 1960, by the Venezuelan Guillermo Morón—*The Political History of José Ortega y Gasset* (Oasis, Mexico D.F., 1960, 207 pages). The work contains the best available account of Ortega's death, and presents a careful reconstruction of Ortega's political development up to the end of the second Spanish republic.

The old Ortega circle that used to meet in the editorial offices of the *Revista de Occidente* in the Calle Braganza in Madrid refused to disband after Ortega's death. This little group of loyal friends and admirers, drawn close together by many a battle in behalf of their dead leader, managed to survive the lean years after Ortega's death. In 1963, after years of patient waiting and unrelenting work in utter privacy, the group succeeded in reestablishing the *Re-*

*vista de Occidente* as a monthly publication on the highest intellectual level. Its editorial staff is dedicated to systematic Ortega studies, and has resisted all temptations to relapse into literary squabbles of the kind that had marked the 1950s.

It borders on the miraculous that the *Revista de Occidente,* Ortega's most important project, could return to life forty years after its first founding, and after a twenty-five-year interval dominated by civil war. Ortega's oldest son, José Ortega y Spottorno, is the titular editor-in-chief, but the real work is done by a team of ten respected scholars guided by Paulino Garagorri, professor of philosophy at the University of Madrid. With its very first issue, the new review achieved distinction. That issue included contributions by Xavier Zubiri, Spain's most famous philosopher next to Ortega, and by Robert Oppenheimer. Later issues contained essays by the French thinkers Louis de Broglie and Denis de Rougemont. In its physical format, too, the new *Revista de Occidente,* is distinguished by handsome design, including those mysterious vignettes in color on white background, now done by the world-famous Spanish painter Antonio Saura.

The new *Revista de Occidente* carries excellent critical reviews of works about Ortega, and, on occasion, original analyses of Ortega's work. Its policy is to avoid controversy with Ortega's conservative opponents. On its pages have appeared many formerly unpublished Ortega letters, and it has offered his entire correspondence with the German historian of literature E. R. Curtius as well as the moving letters written to the young Ortega by the Spanish educator Francisco Giner de los Rios. Progressive theologians such as the German Jesuit Karl Rahner now write in the *Revista de Occidente,* something that would have been inconceivable in the old days. Their contributions appear side by side with those of Marxist scholars such as Herbert Marcuse of the United States or the late Georg Lukács of Hungary. Ortega's friends and disciples find in the *Revista de Occidente* a platform to express their views. Outstanding special issues add to the review's distinction. The resuscitated journal has become an object of pride, though it is perhaps less influential than it was in former days.

Paulino Garagorri is now engaged in preparing an Ortega bibliography, and is preparing for publication hitherto unpublished Ortega papers. He has proved himself to be a supremely independent critic of Ortega studies throughout the world. Among other things he has demonstrated that in the last decade even Ortega's clerical critics have abandoned the "frivolous and malicious attitude" toward Ortega, and that nobody any longer expresses serious doubts about his importance as a philosopher. A study of Ortega's early work, by the Spanish Jesuit Díaz del Cerio, published in 1961, was described as "objective and valuable," while a book by the Chilean Jesuit Larrain Acuna, of 1962, was characterized as "generously conceived and nobly expressed."

Ortega studies have now entered a new phase. Once the subject of criticism based on ignorance or intellectual indifference, he has now become the object of serious investigation and, consequently, of growing appreciation. In Garagorri's words, Ortega has been recognized, at least within the Spanish-speaking world, as a philosopher of "enduring relevance." South American critics, too, give proof that they have overcome their provincialism, and have become participants in the worldwide exchange of ideas.

There, too, Ortega matters, though not, perhaps, as much as in his native Spain.

One unusual item of Ortegiana is a small volume of reminiscences by Manuel, youngest of the three Ortega brothers, issued in 1964. It speaks of "the strong brother's gentle care" that José gave to Manuel, who describes himself as "the weakling brother on the verge of collapse."

The warmest, most personal note is struck in the numerous books and lectures of Julián Marías, whose affection for Ortega has never faltered in three decades. His works contain many personal confessions. He offers the "history of a friendship" that began in 1932, spanned the interruptions of wars and of Ortega's exile, and constituted an "unbroken dialogue" between Ortega and himself that lasted for almost twenty-five years. So close a friendship does lend an important dimension to Marías's work, but carries with it the risk of distorted perspective. Thus, in 1959 Marías's veneration for Ortega prompted him to inflate a passing comment by Ferrater Moras about a "philosophical school of Madrid" into a compendious book (569 pages) with the proud title *The School of Madrid*. This title provoked a number of objections, especially on the part of the Catalan philosophers in exile. He was especially taken to task for the fact that almost a third of the book is devoted to Miguel de Unamuno. For although Unamuno, like García Morente, was personally close to Ortega, founder of this so-called School of Madrid, intellectually they were rather his rivals or even opponents.

Less ambitious in title but even more overpowering in size is Marías's projected three-volume *Ortega,* the first volume of which appeared in 1960. With the aid of a Rockefeller Foundation grant, Marías plans to present Ortega's intellectual biography, and to collect and organize his miscellaneous writings. He proposes to crown the work with a portrayal of "the Ortega who might have been." This would be more than Ortega himself was able to accomplish.

In the *Revista de Occidente,* Garagorri makes it a practice to ignore Ortega's lesser opponents, and to mock the more important ones, among whom are the ultra-conservative Marrero, Argentinian Marxists such as Patricio Canto, or radical pseudo-realists such as Juan Goytisolo, a novelist and essayist residing in Paris. Garagorri likes to remind them that Ortega's political texts did not become available in book form until 1970 (they are in volumes 10 and 11 of the collected works). Ortega's principal works, including the lectures, would fill more than twelves volumes, instead of the eleven we have. Yet Ortega has not left behind even one "regular book." In dealing with such an opus, Garagorri points out, much still remains "to be sorted out, many details remain to be settled." Ortega's work is "still far from being understood, absorbed, or applied in practice." Once that goal is reached, Garagorri claims, the result will be "life on the highest philosophical plane of the entire twentieth century."

Another Ortega scholar must be mentioned, the Jesuit Nemesio González Caminero, a native of Aragon, who teaches the history of philosophy at the Papal University. Author of numerous essays about Ortega, Caminero gained first the acceptance and ultimately the support of Ortega's disciples in Madrid. This broad-minded Jesuit does not hesitate to criticize many of his fellow priests who have attacked Ortega, thus proving once more that the Jesuit order has room for scholarly probity and tolerance. Father

Caminero's differences with Garagorri concerning the various phases in Ortega's intellectual development are minimal, as is his disagreement with Marías concerning the value of Ortega's posthumous book on Leibniz. Father Caminero speaks of Ortega as "the incontestable master of the young generation"—a description that may seem dubious when one thinks of Ortega's exile years. Father Caminero's greatest service to the cause of Ortega is his careful editing of the texts and his appreciation of Ortega as a philosopher of history.

In 1963, another hitherto unpublished body of Ortega material became available: his correspondence with E. R. Curtius, spanning three decades. The Spanish philosopher with a literary talent, and the German literary historian with a philosophical bent, complemented as well as criticized each other. "The two of us draw life not so much from the material world as from an inexhaustible lyricism, an inner stream that is the true fountain of youth," Ortega wrote to Curtius in 1937, from Paris.

It may be noted that the response to Ortega's thought seems to have been most enduring, and also most capricious, in Latin America. A volume of essays *About Ortega* published in Mexico in 1957 by José Gaos, once Ortega's favorite student, remains to this day a treasure trove of information about Ortega's political, prophetic, and patriotic ideas. In Caracas, Manuel Granell, an Ortega champion, undertook a systematic analysis of Ortega's mind. But published in 1960, when the posthumous works were then not yet available, the materials at hand were not sufficient for a full study. He sketched Ortega's intellectual profile but failed to reach his core. Other South American writers on Ortega are Rodríguez Huéscar in Puerto

Rico, Francisco Soler in Chile, and Ferrater Mora and Roura-Parella in the United States. The novelist Francisco Ayala may be reckoned among Ortega's spiritual heirs.

It should not be claimed, however, that twentieth-century Spanish philosophers are all admirers of Ortega. The brilliant Basque Eugenio Imaz, living in exile in Mexico, put on record his opposition to the "Spanish delirium" and the excessive admiration for Ortega, whom he called "the man from Málaga who fancied that he had a German soul." García Bacca, perhaps Spain's most important émigré philosopher, who has lived almost twenty years in Caracas, is the author of many learned books and translations. He makes no more than passing mention of Ortega. Jiménez-Grullón, a Cuban at the University of the Andes in Merida, Mexico, considers Ortega controversial. Basave Fernández del Valle, of Nuevo León University in Monterrey, Mexico, expressed his basic disagreement with Ortega's anthropology and ontology, as did the Cuban Medardo Vitier, who pointed out the contradictions between the early and the later Ortega.

Among the reasons Ortega's influence has not faded to this day are doubtless his vast intellectual curiosity, his vibrant optimism, and his intellectual passion and originality. This holds especially true in the new world. Ortega found fewer complimentary things to say about Latin America than most other visitors from abroad—he spoke of it as condemned to "incurable, infantile primitivism"—yet he has probably elicited more response there than anywhere else.

There is every reason to expect that Latin American thinkers, too, will come to see behind Ortega's "mask," that, discarding the image of Ortega the bullfighter, iconoclast, the braggart of his own originality, they will come to see him as the original, impassioned, profound, optimistic man that in truth he was. Luis Washington Vita of Brazil described Ortega's work as "an instrument enabling us to grasp Brazilian reality on the most diverse planes," and in the pages of *Revista de Occidente* reported at length on Ortega's powerful influence on the legal, aesthetic, political, economic, as well as the philosophical, thinking of Brazil.

There can be no doubt that Ortega's intellectual influence will go on expanding. This growth will be the result of patient scholarly researches rather than of the kind of hero worship that surrounded him, and hampered him, during his life. A German scholar, Udo Rukser, in 1970 called for the establishment of a Center of Ortega Studies to develop the bibliographical research needed to render Ortega's work fully accessible. This seems to be the only way in which Ortega's philosophical thought can be disengaged from its literary and journalistic trimmings and political accidentals, thus revealing its solid and enduring content that to this day is known only partially.

The impressive *Bibliografía de Ortega* (published in *Estudios Ortegianos* No. 5, Madrid: Revista de Occidente, 1971), a volume of 417 pages, was the result of the selfless labors of several dozen Ortega experts from many lands under the editorship of Udo Rukser. It was still in manuscript when Rukser (of Quillota, Chile) died in June 1971, and thus was published only after his death. The work, which took many years to complete and involved an enormous amount of correspondence, was described by Rukser as "complete as far as that is possible, and by far the most extensive bibliography, yet not without gaps and errors." (Another work by Rukser is mentioned in the preface to the *Bibliografía* under the working title *Ortega and German Philosophy.* Excerpts of it were published in various periodicals, and it seems to have been close to completion at the time of Rukser's death, but its fate unfortunately, is still uncertain at this writing.)

No fewer than thirty-seven countries proved to be fertile ground in Rukser's search for Ortega material. Ortega's writings—books, articles, essays, addresses, reviews—have been published in thirty-two of these countries. The section handling publications in Argentina of works by and about Ortega runs to fifty-one pages, taking pride of place even over Spain; the quantity is owing, no doubt, to Ortega's many contributions to Buenos Aires's daily press. The entry for Spain has forty-seven pages, that for Germany, twenty-four, that for the United States, twenty-two.

Within Spanish America, Argentina and Chile have a substantial lead over other countries. According to the number of pages they occupy in Rukser's *Bibliografía,* in descending order, the sequence is as follows: Mexico, Colombia, Venezuela, Peru, and Brazil. Interestingly, countries such as South Africa, Austria, Finland, and Hungary, and even such small nations as Ecuador, El Salvador, and Panama, are represented, and each has been the home of Ortega scholars. Especially revealing is the information from the countries behind the iron curtain and the bamboo curtain: how differently Ortega fared in the two areas can easily be demonstrated. It only confirms our expectations to find that the countries with a relatively higher degree of intellectual freedom have allowed the publication of a greater number of Ortega studies. Yugoslavia, for example, is represented with thirty such studies (and twenty translations of Ortega's works); Cuba offers twenty-four such studies, of which, however, only two were published under Fidel Castro. There follow, in descending order, Communist China (until 1969), Rumania, and the Soviet Union. So vast a country as Soviet Russia has seen only one work of Ortega's in translation—*The Dehumanization of Art*—but, in a period of ten years, allowed the publication of eight studies of the problem of the elite, which is the theme in which the personality of the "bourgeois" or "reactionary" Ortega expressed itself most fully.

The world of learning will have to make peace with the fact that the Ortega whom we will come to know will be more intellectual, therefore more elitist, than the Ortega whom we knew during his lifetime. Ortega will live on as an aristocrat of the mind and will attract only aristocratic followers.

In closing, we recall how Ortega, by precept and example, again and again urged upon the intellectuals of our time the imperative of having the courage to stand alone in the age of the masses that is closing in on us. "The archaic nostalgia for the herd is seizing man," he wrote. "Man is yearning for a shepherd and a sheep dog." But, he went on, we must resist that yearning "by striving to become individuals aiming for the loftiest goals. The human spirit must not be managed like a public utility; men of the spirit, if they wish to carry out their tasks, must once again choose solitude!"

ooo

# Appendix:
# Guide to Ortega's
# Contemporaries

Azaña y Diez, Manuel (1880–1940). Like J. Ruiz Jiménez,
Azaña was educated by the Augustinian monks in the
Escorial. Liberal journalist and writer. Longtime president of the Ateneo in Madrid. Was prime minister of
the second Spanish republic from 1931 to 1933 and in
1936. President of the second Spanish republic in the
republic's last years (1936–39). Died in exile in France.
The posthumous publication of his political diaries
reawakened interest in him.

Azorín (pseudonym of José Martínez Ruiz; 1874–1967).
Novelist, dramatist, and essayist. One of the most sensitive stylists of the famous Generation of '98.

Barea, Arturo (1897–1958). Militant republican. His three-
volume biography, *The Fury of a Rebel* (1951), which
covers his involvement in the early civil war years, has
been translated into many languages.

Baroja y Nessi, Pío (1872–1956). Novelist and essayist. The
most important representative of the Generation of '98.

Calvo Serer, Rafael (born 1916). Professor of philosophy of
history and Spanish philosophy. From 1948 to 1953
he was managing editor of the magazine *Arbor*. Travels

119

and study abroad during the 1960s turned this leading conservative theoretician into a democrat and leftist liberal. In the late 1960s he founded the liberal newspaper *Madrid,* which was forced by the Franco government to suspend publication after lengthy legal struggles. Since the beginning of 1972 he has been in exile in Paris. Wrote essays about the meaning of Spanish history.

Camba, Julio (1882–1962). Journalist, humorist, and satirist. He considered the second Spanish republic as unviably structured for the renewal of Spain.

Costa, Joaquín (1884–1911). Republican politician during the monarchy and political theoretician who worked for agrarian reform. His reform ideas influenced Unamuno, Ortega, and the Generation of '98. His motto was *"regeneración"* and *"europeización."*

D'Ors, Eugenio (1881–1954). Art historian, theoretician, and aesthetician. Wrote extensively on art, history, and culture. In contrast to Ortega, he was conservative and friendly to the government.

Gaos, José (1900–1969). Born in Mexico City. Historian of philosophy. In 1936 was the last rector of the Central University of Madrid. He was a pupil of Ortega, whose teachings he abandoned, rejecting both Ortega's political and philosophical thinking. He eventually turned to agnostic relativism.

García Morente, Manuel (1886–1942). Professor at the Central University of Madrid. Outstanding pedagogue and university reformer. He returned to the faith of his youth while in exile in Argentina, being ordained at the age of fifty-four.

Giner de los Ríos, Francisco (1839–1915). Most important student of Sanz del Río, founder of the Institución Libre de Enseñanza. A leader of the *krausistas* around the turn of the century. Outstanding, nonconformist, progressive pedagogue and humanist, whose interests ranged from law to general cultural areas, as can be seen in his numerous "Estudios." The school he founded, Estudios, has existed in Madrid for about a hundred years.

Herrera y Oria, Angel (1886–1968). Leading journalist. Ordained in 1940. Became bishop of Málaga in 1947. His attempt to create a strong Christian-democratic party failed. He became a theologian while living abroad. On his return to Spain he kept aloof from politics and worked again as a priest and a social educator and reformer.

Iglesias, Pablo (1850–1925). President of the Printing Union of Madrid. Founder of the Spanish socialist workers' party. A friend of Benito Pérez Galdós.

Jiménez, Juan Ramón (1881–1958). One of Spain's outstanding poets. Winner of the Nobel Prize in 1956. During the civil war he took refuge in the United States, finally settling in Puerto Rico, where he died.

Laín Entralgo, Pedro (born 1908). Physician and historian, he was also committed to the literary and the philosophical. He was politically oriented to the left but became, in his middle years, a leader of the Falangists.

Lerroux, Alejandro (1864–1949). Journalist and liberal politician and parliamentarian. Radically anticlerical. In the second Spanish republic he was president from 1934 to 1935 with the support of the Christian-democratic party. Popular but not respected. Considered a demagogue by many.

Madariaga, Salvador de (born 1886). Diplomat and historian. During exile he was president of the Liberal World Union. Famous for his extensive and important literary and historical oeuvre.

Maeztu, Ramiro de (1874–1936). Journalist and essayist. With Azorín and Pío Baroja y Nessi, he was one of the pioneers of the Generation of '98. He was hated as a monarchist politician for his activity as critic of the republic and prior to that as ambassador to Argentina under Primo de Rivera. He and Calvo Sotelo were assassinated at the outbreak of the civil war in 1936 in Madrid. Today he is counted among Spain's political martyrs.

Marañón, Gregorio (1887–1960). Physician, historian, politician, and essayist.

Marías, Julian (born 1914). A student of Ortega. Left Spain because of his opposition to the Franco regime. Has been visiting professor at Harvard, Yale, and the University of Puerto Rico. Author of a history of philosophy. He is committed to systematizing and expanding Ortega's ideas in his projected three-volume *Ortega*.

Marrero, Vicente (born ca. 1922). Started his career as lawyer and then turned to philosophical writing. Severe critic of Ortega and his followers.

Maura, Antonio (1853–1925). Liberal politician, who turned conservative. Between 1903 and 1922 he was prime minister five times.

Menéndez y Pelayo, Marcelino (1856–1912). Literary historian. Fought as cultural historian against the anticlerical reformers of his time. Professor at the Central University of Madrid for twenty years. Director of the National Library. Under Franco venerated as the standardbearer of the traditionalists.

Menéndez Pidal, Ramón (1869–1969). Spain's most outstanding philologist. From 1925 on he was president of the Real Academia de la Lengua.

Nicol, Eduardo (born 1907). Professor of philosophy in Barcelona. Has lived in Mexico since 1940.

Ortega Munilla, José (1856–1922). Influential Madrid journalist and novelist. Chief editor of *Imparcial*, the leading newspaper.

Pérez de Ayala, Ramón (1881–1962). Novelist and critic. Anglophile. Ambassador to the Court of St. James.

Primo de Rivera, José Antonio (1903–36). Son of the dictator-general. Founded the Falangist movement in October 1933, an umbrella group of several trends among students and workers. Incorporated ideas of Costa, Menéndez y Pelayo, Ortega, and Mussolini. Assassinated by republicans in 1936.

Primo de Rivera, Miguel (1870–1930). As commanding general in Barcelona he issued a manifesto on 12 September 1923 against parliament, thus suspending the constitution and proclaiming a military directorate. The coup was accepted by King Alfonso XIII. During the six years of dictatorship, economic and social progress was made, but he alienated the intellectuals (Ortega, Unamuno, among others) and politicians by his censorship regulations. He finally also lost the support of the military elite. He was deposed in 1929 by Alfonso under pressure by many factions. In 1930 the "charitable benign despot" died alone in Paris.

Ruiz Jiménez, Joaquín (born 1913). Professor of law at the University of Salamanca. Ambassador to the Vatican, 1951–56. Minister of education. He was the son of a liberal minister under Alfonso XIII. Catholic student leader. Under Franco turned more and more into an opposition democrat and became an outspoken opponent of Franco. His important magazine *Diálogo* was critical of the regime, and was several times forced to suspend publication.

Salmerón, Nicolás (1838–1908). Philosopher, exponent of *krausismo*, militant republican. In 1873 he was second president of the first Spanish republic. Supporter of the Institución Libre de Enseñanza, the force in Spanish cultural life that was independent of state and church and led to the establishment of the second republic.

Tovar Llorente, Antonio (born 1911). Translator and editor of ancient texts. Professor and later rector (1951–56) at the University of Salamanca. In the 1960s he became a critic of the Franco regime and left Spain. Now professor of Basque at the University of Tübingen.

Unamuno, Miguel de (1864–1936). Philosopher, novelist, essayist, and dramatist. Professor and later chancellor of the University of Salamanca. His critical opposition to all forms of dogmatism brought him into conflict with the dominant parties and resulted in political persecution and condemnation by the church. He was exiled from 1924 to 1930 during the dictatorship of Primo de Rivera.

Valle-Inclán, Ramón (1869–1936). Novelist, poet, and dramatist.

Zaragüeta, Juan (born 1883). Basque lay priest. Professor of neo-Thomistic philosophy, pedagogy, psychology, and metaphysics at the Central University of Madrid.

Zubiri, Xavier (born 1898). Outstanding theologian and philosopher.

○○○○○○○○○○○○○○○○○○○○○○○○○○○○○○○○○○○○○○○○○○○○○○○○

# *Bibliography*

## *1. Works by Ortega y Gasset*

*Meditaciones del Quijote,* 1914. Translation: *Meditations on Quixote,* 1961.

*Vieja y nueva política,* 1914.

*Personas, obras y cosas,* 1916.

*España invertebrada,* 1922. Translation: *Invertebrate Spain,* 1937.

*El tema de nuestro tiempo,* 1923. Translation: *The Modern Theme,* 1933.

*Ni vitalismo ni racionalismo,* 1924.

*La deshumanización del arte,* 1925. Translation: *The Dehumanization of Art,* 1948.

*Ideas sobre la novela,* 1925. Translation: *Notes on the Novel,* 1948.

*¿Qué es filosofía?,* 1929. Translation: *What Is Philosophy?,* 1960.

*La rebelión de las masas,* 1930. Translation: *Revolt of the Masses,* 1932.

*La redención de las provincias y la decadencia nacional,* 1931.

125

*Rectificación de la república,* 1931.

*Pidiendo un Goethe desde dentro,* 1932.

*Misión de la universidad,* 1932. Translation: *Mission of the University,* 1966.

*En torno a Galileo,* 1933. Translation: *Man and Crisis,* 1958.

*Ensimismamiento y alteración,* 1939.

*Estudios sobre el amor,* 1939. Translation: *On Love,* 1957.

*Ideas y creencias,* 1940.

*Historia como sistema,* 1941. Translation: *History as a System,* 1936.

*Teoría de Andalucía y otros ensayos,* 1942.

*Del imperio romano,* 1946. Translation: *Concord and Liberty,* 1963.

*Obras completas,* 6 vols., 1946ff. Enlarged edition, 9 vols., 1957.

*Papeles sobre Velázquez y Goya,* 1950.

*El hombre y la gente,* 1957. Translation: *Man and People,* 1957.

*La idea de principio en Leibniz y la evolución de la teoría deductiva,* 1958.

*Prólogo para alemanes,* 1959.

## 2. About Ortega y Gasset

Barea, Arturo. In *Books Abroad,* Spring 1953.

Bentley, Eric. In *Saturday Review,* 23 December 1944.

Brinton, Crane. In *Saturday Review,* 15 April 1941.

Fernández de la Mora, Gonzalo. *Ortega y el 98.* Madrid, 1961.

Ferrater Mora, José. *Ortega y Gasset: An Outline of His Philosophy.* New Haven: Yale University Press, 1957.

Gaos, José. *Sobre Ortega y Gasset.* México D. F., 1957.

Garagorri, Paulino. *Unamuno, Ortega, Zubiri en la filosofía española*. Madrid, 1968.

Marañón, Gregorio. *Acto en memoria del catedrático Don José Ortega y Gasset*. Madrid: University of Madrid, 1955.

Marías, Julián. *José Ortega y Gasset: Circumstance and Vocation*. Translated by Frances M. López-Morillas. Norman: University of Oklahoma Press, 1970.

Morón, Guillermo. *Historia política de José Ortega y Gasset*. México D. F., 1960.

Oromí, Miguel. *Ortega y la filosofía, seis glosas*. Madrid: Esplandián, 1953.

Read, Herbert. "High Noon and Darkest Night: Some Observations on Ortega y Gasset's philosophy of Art." *Journal of Aesthetics and Art Criticism* 23 (1964):43–50.

Rukser, Udo, ed. *Bibliografía de Ortega*. In *Estudios Ortegianos*, No. 5. Madrid: Revista de Occidente, 1971.

Sánchez Villaseñor, José, S. J. *Ortega y Gasset: Existentialist*. Chicago, 1949.

Vela, Fernando. *Ortega y los existencialismos*. Madrid, 1961.

Weber, F. "An Approach to Ortega's Idea of Culture." *Hispanic Review* 32 (1964):142–56.

Winecoff, J. "José Ortega y Gasset: Existentialist?" *Dissertation Abstracts* 22 (1962):4357.

# Index

---

*Spanish names are listed in this index by the patronymic,
that is, the first name in a compound surname. Thus, the
references to Federico García Lorca, for example, are listed
under García.*